'We must judge a man, according to Beyle, neither by what he says, nor by what he writes. I add: nor by what he does'
ALBERT CAMUS, *Notebook VI*

'Faith can move mountains, but it won't beat a fast draw'
FROM *El Dorado* (1967)

Chapter One

The first flush of daylight was lining the eastern sky as Flight RG723 said goodbye to its fighter escort and swung into the landing pattern, bringing him home for the last time. Already his people were gathering along the expressway from the airport through the suburbs, a million of them or more, carrying their flags and banners, preparing their tears of welcome and lamentation as the big jet came out of the rising sun into São Paulo.

Eleven hours out of Paris, Captain Gomes Pinto floated the McDonnell-Douglas M D11 and its strange cargo over the endless clusters of high-rise blocks with their shanty-town infills. São Paulo may be one of the biggest and ugliest cities on earth, a vast megalopolis of extreme wealth and extreme poverty, but in that dawn its inhabitants turned into villagers, sharing in the mourning for their golden boy, their favourite son, their champion.

At 6.12 a.m. the plane touched down on the main runway of Guaralhos airport. Its passengers, restricted to the economy compartment, disembarked. Over the next thirty minutes the polished mahogany casket containing the mortal remains of Ayrton Senna was removed from the business-class section, lowered to the ground on an electric lift, and carried by soldiers of the Polícia da Aeronáutica to a waiting fire-engine, where it was draped with the *bandeira*, the familiar green and yellow national flag of Brazil. At 6.45 a.m. under a sky already bright blue, the fire-engine moved off, preceded by an arrowhead of seventeen police outriders in white leathers who led the motorcade on the thirty-kilometre journey into the city.

Just beyond the airport perimeter, the taxi driver found a gap to park on the already crowded grass verge. We jumped out and ran up the slope to join the people lining the six-lane highway, just

1

in time to see the parade go by. On the rear deck of the fire-engine, a quartet of white-capped cadets from the Military Police school sat on either side of the coffin, facing fore and aft, mounting guard; five more clung to the ledge at the rear of the vehicle. Behind it, in the slipstream of the spectators' applause, came the official cars and the police vans. As soon as they had passed, the taxi driver and I slid back down the steep grass slope, got back into the car, and immediately found ourselves sucked into the wedge of unofficial traffic following the motorcade.

It was a vast dusty mass numbering hundreds of vehicles in all shapes and sizes and states of repair, battered Beetles and shiny Subarus, smart new XR3s and heavily oversubscribed jeeps, taxis and pick-ups, a Mack truck flying a Brazilian flag the size of a house, all crossing and recrossing the central reservation, some racing headlong down the wrong side of the carriageway in an attempt to keep up with Ayrton Senna's last ride. Most of the cars had his photograph taped inside the windscreen, or black scarves tied to the radio aerial. One car-borne banner, hastily hand-lettered, read *Adeus Ayrton – Tricampeão*. Farewell, Ayrton – triple champion. From many side-windows, in an echo of Senna's trademark gesture on so many afternoons of triumph around the world, a spare hand held a *bandeira*, its colours stiffened in the airstream.

Witnesses to this spectacle, this *Mad Max* remake of a grand prix lap of honour, the people of Ayrton Senna's home town thronged the pavements and overpasses and windows and parapets of their crumbling concrete canyons, applauding the passage of their champion and shedding neither the first nor the last of their tears. Motorcycles and pushbikes joined the parade. As the day's rush hour began, the weight of extra traffic choked the city. Sometimes, like the people in the blocked-off side roads, we had to stop and switch off the engine, getting out and turning our faces to the sky, where a dozen police and television helicopters hovered and circled, marking the motorcade's progress like a cloud of midsummer midges.

2

As we passed through the Anhangabau tunnel, a group of bikers set up a chant: 'Olé, olé, olé, olé, Senna.' Now banners and freshly sprayed graffiti were everywhere, dangled from every bridge, painted on every blank surface: '*Obrigado Senna*' (thank you, Senna), '*Senna não morreu, porque os deuses não morrem*' (Senna isn't dead, because gods don't die). And '*Obrigado, Senna por fazer nossos domingos felizes*' (thank you, Senna, for making our Sundays so happy).

As it neared its destination, the procession slowed. The motorcycle outriders peeled away, replaced by an honour guard of mounted lancers: five at the front on white horses, two dozen more on bays with red cockades on their black steel helmets, flanking the fire-engine as it crawled between crowds now twenty deep, jammed together, their arms outstretched above their heads, applauding Senna's passage.

Beneath the pink blossom of the late-blooming *paneira* trees, I walked round the July 9 Palace, the state legislative assembly building, a classic of fifties concrete brutalism set within a city park in São Paulo's southern zone. All the way round, tens of thousands of people were already waiting calmly in line. Inside, before the doors were opened, a private twenty-minute religious ceremony was conducted by Pastor Sabatini Lali in the presence of Senna's family, gathered around the coffin. By the time the doors of the Monumental Hall were opened to the public, the queue of those wishing to pay their last respects was at least three miles long, winding back up the drive, out through the entrance and around the perimeter of the compound, snaking back and forth, unsupervised but in perfect order, through the park. It would take those at the back of the queue seven hours to reach their goal, shuffling slowly forward in what, by the middle of the morning, had become eighty-degree heat, to salute the casket, now with a fresh *bandeira* coverlet and surmounted by one of Senna's old helmets, the display guarded by two soldiers with pikes and four riflemen, their weapons reversed.

Upon hearing the news of Sunday afternoon's tragedy at the

Imola autodrome, President Itamar Franco had immediately declared three days of national mourning, including a day off for all state schools. So Brazilians of all ages and types came to Ibirapuera Park to say a personal farewell. Among the first in line was Adelia Scott, eighty-four years old, who had travelled many hours from her home in the south of the country. 'I adored him,' she said. Near her at the head of the queue was a thirteen-year-old schoolboy, Marco Putnoki, who had been in line since the previous afternoon. In fact the vast majority of those queuing to say farewell were under twenty-five, which said something about both Ayrton Senna and Brazil.

Senna was young and beautiful in a country where those assets have often seemed to represent the only stable currency, and the naked distress of the young mourners – university students and McDonald's workers alike – showed very starkly what he had meant to them. 'He was our hero,' said eighteen-year-old Silvia Barros, 'our only one.'

At a discreet rear entrance, family, friends, business associates and racing colleagues were arriving to pay their respects, each with a small stick-on lapel badge bearing a single letter: F for *familia*, A for *amigos*. Among the As was twenty-three-year-old Christian Fittipaldi, a member of Brazil's foremost motor-racing dynasty and in his second season of Formula One. I asked him to explain the dead man's special significance to his country's young people. 'He was a good example to everyone,' Fittipaldi said. 'He was someone you always looked to, and not only on the track. You know, if a country has a lot of political and economic problems, and it has someone who does so well, who goes out into the world to represent a Third World country and succeeds against people from places where the conditions are very much better . . . well, he was a big plus for us, that's all.' Fittipaldi turned away to comfort his grand prix colleague and fellow countryman Rubens Barrichello, who had broken off an interview with a television reporter and was weeping openly on a friend's shoulder.

Back out by the main gate, the mood of restraint was breaking down in the face of a growing crush, funnelled by police through a small entrance. More than 150 people fainted as the riot squad of the military police attempted to restore order beneath a banner that gave some idea of the strength of feeling Senna's death had aroused among his people. 'Assassinos Mercenários Queremos Justiça' it read, in stark black and red lettering: money-grabbing assassins, the people demand justice.

Hour after hour the young and old filed by, thousand upon thousand, given just enough time to glance quickly across at the little grandstand crammed with press photographers and TV cameramen, their telephoto lenses trained on the small VIP enclosure opposite, anxious not to miss the visits by family, friends, colleagues and celebrities – by his father, Milton da Silva, his mother, Neyde, his brother, Leonardo, and his sister, Viviane; by President Itamar, with the entire cast of São Paulo's political life; by his personal pilot, Captain Owen O'Mahony; and by the footballer Viola, who had dedicated his goal for Brazil against Iceland in Florianopolis the previous night to the dead man's memory and now wore the colours of his club, Corinthians, which Senna had supported. (The following night, Viola would score twice for the club in a league match against Guarani, and on both occasions would celebrate by running a lap of his home stadium holding a small *bandeira* in his hand, past banners that read 'Senna – in our hearts for ever' and 'Thank you, Ayrton'.)

Senna's girlfriend, Adriane Galisteu, a blonde twenty-one-year-old former singer and fashion model, slipped in and out; they had spent the last thirteen months together, mostly at his home in Faro, on the southernmost tip of Portugal, and at his beach house outside São Paulo. Her visit to her lover's remains coincided with the appearances of Alain Prost, Senna's oldest and bitterest adversary, and Gerhard Berger, his best friend in the paddock. Both embraced her, enfolding her distress inside their own. Frank Williams, the entrant of the car in which Senna had died three days previously, arrived in his wheelchair, his drawn face betraying his grief. Ron Dennis, the owner of the McLaren team, with whom Senna had won his three world championships, sat on the VIP bench for forty silent minutes. Nuno Cobra, for ten years Senna's personal physiotherapist and counsellor, fine-featured and spare-framed, walked haltingly across to the silver catafalque and wept as he stroked the head of the coffin, addressing it with tender words, as though he were trying to console an unhappy child. Those of us watching at that moment had to turn our eyes away from such sadness.

In more normal circumstances the coffin would have been open, the face of the deceased available to the last parting gaze of the bereaved. But so grievous had been the injuries caused to Senna's skull in the crash at the Imola autodrome three days earlier that the conventional cosmetic preparation was abandoned and, at the family's request, the lid stayed shut. Still, many of those who passed by in a ceaseless flow blew kisses at the coffin, or gave it a poignant little wave, or crossed themselves, or moved their lips in a silent farewell prayer. Others could do little beyond clutch each other in grief, one or two giving way altogether and collapsing into the arms of waiting paramedics. Over the rope separating them from the coffin they dropped keepsakes – a single flower, a bracelet, a poem. Some held up photographs of the great man as they passed. One older woman had a scrap of paper pinned to her T-shirt, with a scrawled message: '*Senna obrigado*'. Thank you, Senna. Again and again, that was said. Thank you for what you gave us. A man of advanced years halted, threw his arms wide, and began a formal valedictory address to the coffin before being gently cut short and moved on by an attendant. In the late afternoon, a blind man in a business suit passed by, led by a friend; he, too, had spent seven hours in line.

A high proportion of the younger people – the girls, mostly – had the dead man's name written with felt-tip pen across their foreheads. Even more of them had three stripes painted on each cheek, in the colours of yellow, green and black. A Brazilian friend walked me out of the building and into the park, explaining as we passed the line of mourners that this custom had begun two years earlier, when the youth of the country took to the streets for the first time in twenty years to demand the impeachment and removal of the corrupt president Collor de Mello. 'They painted themselves with a yellow stripe and a green stripe, the colours of Brazil,' Ana Cecília said. 'Now they've added a black stripe, for mourning.'

Leaving the hall, going back into the sunshine, we passed by an avenue of floral tributes piled high between the walkways. Giant constructions of exotic blooms, floral crosses and flags and wheels, some bearing satin sashes lettered with the titles of official organizations and companies with which Senna had dealings, others with cards signed by private individuals. Wreaths from Goodyear, from Audi, from São Paulo and Corinthians football clubs, from the Fittipaldi family, from the Andrettis – Mario and Dee, Michael and Sandra – and from Bernie Ecclestone and the Formula One Constructors' Association. Flowers from automobile clubs around Brazil and Senna fan clubs around the world. Two huge crosses, from Mansour and Kathy Ojjeh of TAG, among his sponsors in the championship years, and from McLaren International; these were people who had paid him a million dollars a race, and been happy to do so. And a plain circlet of white chrysanthemums 'from two of your many fans in Northern Ireland'.

In a room deep within the July 9 Palace, Senna's brother, Leonardo Senna da Silva, was cutting across the elegiac mood, addressing a press conference with angry words which spoke of another aspect of the tragedy, one that would reverberate with growing intensity over the coming months. 'The motor sport authorities are only interested in money,' he was saying, echoing the angry banner at the main gate. They knew the dangers, the risks the drivers were facing at Imola, the fact that at the corner called Tamburello, where Senna had died, only a narrow strip of grass and twenty metres of tarmac separated the track from a solid concrete wall. If they'd

7

taken the correct precautions, Leonardo told reporters, his face held taut to conceal the depth of his emotions, 'my brother would be alive today'.

Outside, in the afternoon heat, more banners had been hung on the railings of the perimeter fence: '*Senna obrigado*', '*Adeus Senna*', '*Senna tricampeão*', '*Senna o melhor*'. A few of them bore no name, but simply a single word: *saudade*. 'It's the most beautiful word in the Portuguese language,' my friend Ana Cecília said as we bought a couple of bottles of mineral water from a vendor by the palace fence. 'And it's one of those for which there's no direct translation. It means the sense of loss and sadness you feel when the person you love isn't there any more. No other language has this word.'

All through the night they passed in and out of the Monumental Hall. An hour after dawn, 300 kilometres down the Atlantic coast, in the city of Curitiba, a sixteen-year-old student switched off the early morning television news coverage of the obsequies and shot herself with a .22 calibre revolver. 'I'm killing myself because I don't want to suffer any more,' Zuleika da Costa Rosa wrote in a last note to her parents and her ex-boyfriend. 'I'm going to meet Ayrton Senna. With love to you and to Fabrício. Goodbye, mother and father.'

By ten o'clock, when the howitzers of the 2nd Artillery Brigade fired a twenty-one-gun salute over Ibirapuera Park, more than 200,000 people had paid their last respects in person. Now rose petals were strewn over the coffin and its enveloping flag as cadets of the Barro Branco military academy hoisted it off the catafalque and on to their shoulders, carrying it out of the hall and down the path between the floral tributes to the waiting fire-engine.

This second and final motorcade, along fifteen kilometres of city and suburban streets to the Morumbi cemetery, was itself watched and accompanied by something like a quarter of a million people. More banners and placards were out, broadcasting the now familiar litany: '*Ayrton Senna para sempre*', '*Adeus*', '*Valeu*', '*Obrigado*'. And this, in translation: 'You were worth more than 90 per cent of our politicians.' Outside the Beethoven Academy of Music on the Avenida Reboucas, a pianist performed the music customarily used by TV Globo, the Brazilian network, to celebrate Senna's victories. Ana Cecília, who was not particularly a fan of motor racing, cried when she heard its evocation of his years of glory, and of what his success had meant to her country.

Around Brazil, tens of millions more watched on television as the seven planes of the Esquadrilha de Fumaça – the Brazilian air force aerobatic display team – laid smoke trails in diamond formation as the cortege crawled up the incline to Morumbi, an enclave of affluence set high above the city. The last kilometre of steeply winding road looked like the Alpe d'Huez on Tour de France day, lined with people applauding and holding out messages as the parade went by. The difference was that many of these people were weeping, even as their hands applauded the passage of their champion. 'This manifestation says everything,' the state governor paused to announce, 'about the high level of affection and respect the people have for their hero.' I hadn't seen anything like it since the funeral of Bob Marley in 1981, when a similar motorcade chased from one side of Jamaica to another, tracked by helicopters and watched by thousands of ordinary people as their hero – who had been one of them, the same flesh and dreams – made his last passage through their towns and villages.

But Senna's final resting place was very different from Marley's tiny brick mausoleum on a hill in a remote rural hamlet, his birthplace. We waited for Senna behind guarded walls and overlooked by luxury high-rise apartment blocks in the Cemitério de Morumbi, a round park as big as a dozen football pitches. No headstones on these graves: the flat expanse of bright green was broken only by small engraved plaques laid into the grass, their wide dispersal the clearest possible evidence of the wealth buried here, an eloquent expression of privilege in a teeming city where hundreds of thousands are wedged together to live and die in improvised shanties.

We watched the official mourners arrive, the little Fs and As affixed to their dark suits and black silk mourning frocks. They came in limousines, in mini-coaches and in helicopters which shuttled to and fro, landing on an improvised pad behind a small copse, their security assured by members of the Grupo de Ações Táticas Especiais, the Brazilian special forces unit, in matt grey combat uniforms and black baseball caps, holsters slung low and strapped down on their hips. We stood and made notes while small groups of relatives and friends walked slowly up a rope-lined pathway of pale green carpeting to the middle of the circular central lawn, where brighter green tarpaulins lay around the freshly dug grave and a small white canopy cast shade over the spot where the ceremony was about to take place.

Eventually there would be 500 or so in attendance. At the centre, the close-knit family: father, mother, sister, brother. The lovers: Adriane Galisteu, arriving with a friend, Birgit Sauer, wife of the former head of Volkswagen Brazil; and her predecessor, Xuxa Meneghel, the popular singer and television presenter, ensconced in the family group. The friends: the boxer Adilson Maguila Rodrigues, the artists Francisco Cuoco and Alberto Riccelli. On the periphery, the Italian ambassador and the president of the Italian automobile federation, patiently answering reporters' questions about whether Senna had been killed because Imola was unsafe. The Formula One bosses: Ken Tyrrell, the doyen; Peter Collins of Lotus, the team with which Senna had won his first grand prix; Frank Williams, in whose car he had died, sensitive to the feelings of the Brazilian fans and arriving in a van with the curtains drawn; and Ron Dennis of McLaren, making his entrance surrounded by the cast of *Reservoir Dogs*, silent and compactly built men in black suits and Ray-Bans.

A distant humming in the skies announced the approach of the procession. As half a dozen TV network helicopters appeared over the horizon, the 2nd Guards Battalion of the Southeastern Military Command straightened their green uniforms and shouldered their rifles, forming ranks just inside the cemetery gates.

Nearby, in the same shaded area, the pallbearers assembled: Gerhard Berger, outwardly calm but occasionally turning aside to recover his composure; Alain Prost and Michele Alboreto, veterans of many battles with the dead man; the former triple champion Jackie Stewart, representing not just his own era but all those that had gone before; Damon Hill, Senna's last team mate, behind dark glasses, like all of the Fittipaldi clan – Emerson, Wilson and Christian; fellow Brazilians Rubens Barrichello, Maurizio Sandro Sala, Roberto Moreno and Raul Boesel; Pedro Lamy, a young Portuguese driver befriended by Senna when he came into Formula One as a novice with the Lotus team; Derek Warwick, whom Senna had once notoriously vetoed as his team mate; Johnny Herbert, the Lotus driver; Thierry Boutsen, of Belgium, a quiet man and a close friend who, with his wife, had often stayed with Senna and Adriane at the villa on the Algarve; and Hans-Joachim Stuck, the tall German whose father had raced before the war, in the golden age.

Prost, the reigning world champion, was the magnet for the TV cameras and radio microphones, and he obliged the newsmen's requests to talk about Senna's accident. 'I was shocked,' he said. 'He was the kind of guy you really think it won't happen to. He was the master of his job. For sure, something happened with the car. Motor racing is always dangerous, but we must minimize the risks wherever possible. I think it's time for changing a lot of things. It's not a question of rules. It's a question of philosophy, of whether you have respect for the drivers.'

He talked a bit about how, after five years of conflict, he and Senna had become reconciled in the Brazilian's final days, their growing warmth towards each other culminating in an embrace at Imola on the eve of the crash. Nobody wanted to doubt Prost's sincerity, but it seemed a bit pat, somehow, a bit too scripted for comfort. After all, these two men had developed a rivalry that went

11

beyond the fight for a mere race or even a championship, deep into complex questions of integrity and manhood, dragging us along with them, making us take sides and argue cases.

But what the journalists really wanted to know was whether, in the cold-blooded way of the Formula One world, Prost planned to annul his recent retirement and step back into the car from which Senna had ousted him with such public rancour only a few months earlier. 'Out of respect for him,' Prost declared, 'I would never, never, never take the seat in his car.'

If you stood back and watched this little *tableau vivant*, this gaggle of reporters and cameramen engulfing a small curly-haired figure, suddenly it looked like all those Fridays and Saturdays in paddocks and pit lanes around the world, when men and women with notebooks and cameras would cluster around Prost and Senna at the end of a practice session. The two drivers would be perhaps twenty yards apart, each telling the story of the day from his own point of view and in his own characteristic style, but each really talking as much about the other as about himself – even though, in Senna's case, the rivalry ran so deep that he could not bring himself to utter his adversary's name.

Now, in this grassy paddock, there was just the one cluster. 'We were enemies at one stage,' Prost was saying, 'but very close at the same time because we were fighting against each other, and the longer it went on the closer we became. For ten years it was Prost and Senna. Now it's just Prost. Half of my career has gone today.'

Among the drivers who had played significant roles in Senna's career, there were three notable absentees, two of them former world champions and the third a champion to come. The first, Nigel Mansell, who beat Senna to the title in 1992, was busy with his new career in America, preparing for his second attempt on the Indy 500 at the end of May. A couple of weeks after the funeral, sitting in his team's caravan at the Indianapolis Motor Speedway, Mansell would talk quietly and with obvious feeling about Senna's death. The Englishman tries hard to be a good public relations man, but seldom on behalf of others, and to say he lacks a certain smoothness of tongue would be an understatement; which is perhaps why his regret seemed convincing.

The other missing champion, Nelson Piquet, had won three world titles, just like Senna. But he had been comprehensively replaced in Brazilian hearts by the younger man several years earlier, and had taken it badly. Now, perhaps to his credit, he refused to dissemble, unable to pretend that he had not publicly insulted Senna by referring to him as 'the São Paulo taxi driver', and much worse. Nevertheless his remarks seemed pointless, reflecting more on his own lack of mature judgement than on Senna's character. 'I've never liked going to funerals,' Piquet said. 'Besides, I didn't want to act like Prost did, pretending he was Senna's friend when they had actually spent all their lives fighting with each other.'

A lesser-known Brazilian grand prix driver, Chico Serra, shared his feelings. 'I didn't turn up for the funeral because I didn't want to get upset,' Serra said. 'There was too much pretence, which made me sick. Some people came a long way just to use the situation for their own good. These people never helped him, and they wanted to make us believe that they were great friends who were suffering so much. Going to the funeral was more beneficial to them than winning at Indianapolis.' Serra's bitter words were lent an extra resonance by the knowledge that it was he, twelve years earlier, who had set the young Ayrton Senna's car-racing career in motion by taking him to England and arranging his first drive. Serra himself fiddled around at the back of the Formula One field for two or three seasons in the early eighties, watching his protégé catch him up and then overtake.

The third absentee was Michael Schumacher, the man who had been expected to replace Senna as the presiding genius of Formula One, the greatest talent of his generation, the standard-setter. Most people expected it to take another season or two, and perhaps even Senna's retirement, for the succession to be confirmed. But Schumacher had unexpectedly beaten Senna in the first two races of the 1994 season, and his car had been only a few yards behind when Senna left the track at Imola and died. Now he preferred to concentrate on his preparations for the next race, at Monaco.

Other people, not among Senna's former rivals on the track, were missing from the ceremonies, in particular two English administrators of Formula One: Max Mosley, president of the Fédération Internationale de l'Automobile, and therefore ultimately responsible for circuit safety standards; and Bernie Ecclestone, boss of the Formula One Constructors' Association, thought to be implicated in the confusion over delaying the announcement of Senna's death in order to get the San Marino Grand Prix restarted. Ecclestone's role was the subject of intense and bitter speculation among ordinary Brazilians, whose powerful feeling was that if Senna had indeed died instantly, the race should have been cancelled out of respect and common humanity. Ecclestone had been sighted in a São Paulo hotel that morning but stayed away, having been informed by Leonardo Senna da Silva that his presence would be 'inconvenient'. For his part, Ecclestone issued a communiqué announcing that he would be meeting the state governor that afternoon to discuss the accident.

But now the drivers, their faces bleak beyond words, set the coffin moving on its metal trolley. After fifty yards they stopped, opposite the guardsmen, who pointed their automatic weapons at the ground and, on a shouted order, fired three volleys in salute. Between each fusillade, the tinkling of empty brass shells on the asphalt could be heard over the background throb of the rotor blades circling high above. Then, surrounded by a hideous scrimmage of photographers, the drivers guided Senna down the drive to the lawn, where the casket was taken over by a dozen police cadets, who carried it up the pathway to the grave as the drivers joined the group around the grave. A hundred yards away, by the cemetery gates, a couple of boys were on their hands and knees among the ranks of guardsmen, collecting the spent shells from the salute.

In the front row by the open grave were the dead man's immediate family: his mother, father, sister, brother, nephew and nieces. Behind them were the seats reserved for Adriane Galisteu and her most famous predecessor in Senna's affections, Xuxa Meneghel. But even now there were signs of tension, small ripples betraying darker undercurrents of feeling. When Adriane took her place in the second row, Xuxa rose quickly and moved elsewhere.

The ceremony lasted half an hour under a bright midday sun, and only two voices were heard: those of Pastor Lali and Senna's beloved sister Viviane, who clutched the helmet that had rested on the coffin during the lying in state as she gave a final address over the grave, speaking both of her brother and their country.

'Brazil is going through a very bad time,' she told the standing congregation. 'No one feels like helping anyone any more. People just live for themselves. My brother had a mission, and our family is in deep emotion today because we didn't realize it had made him so greatly loved. I saw how the ordinary people showed their feelings. Some of them were shoeless; others were dressed in silk. He united them, even through his death.' The noise from the steel blades of the helicopters chopped at her words, but she continued, and even those with no command of Portuguese could follow the gestures. 'I think that my brother is not down there,' she said, pointing to the earth, 'but up in the heavens.' And as she spoke, two planes from the aerobatic team traced a big heart and a giant S in white smoke on the bright blue canvas high above the cemetery.

Finally Viviane threw up her right arm, in imitation of her brother's victory salute. '*Valeu Senna,*' she cried. And her listeners responded: '*Valeu Senna.*' Farewell.

The mourners remained by the graveside for long minutes, talking in small huddles that blended and dispersed and regrouped. Gradually they began to move, saying their farewells, walking slowly across the grass and down the pathways, back to the helicopters and limousines. Adriane Galisteu made to enter one of the family cars but was told there was no seat for her and left with her friend Birgit, destiny uncertain. (Later, by her own account, during a final visit to Senna's São Paulo apartment, she was to ask his mother only for his toothbrush and the pyjamas he wore on their last night together.) In contrast, Xuxa walked away from the grave shoulder to shoulder with Viviane, riding out in the family limousine, clearly endorsed as the official widow.

And as the helicopters rose and the limousines sighed away, a van drove across the grass up to the graveside. Two men in overalls climbed out and began to unload its contents, the flowers from the hall back in Ibirapuera Park. As they started to heap them around the grave, Ana Cecília and I walked across the grass to have a look. New among them was a fresh wreath with a card handwritten in capital letters: 'Dear Ayrton, Rest well. You deserve it. You're still the hero and will remain so for many of us. We will always remember you. Love, Tina Turner.'

By half-past one, the mourners had left the Cemitério de Morumbi. The workmen were now arranging the flowers more carefully around the grave, making sure piles of blooms did not obscure a small bronze plaque laid into the freshly pressed turf. It read: *Ayrton Senna da Silva 21.3.1960–1.5.94. Nada pode me separar do amor de Deus.* Nothing can separate me from the love of God.

Almost twenty-four hours earlier, a small boy had passed in front of the coffin in the hall of the July 9 Palace and, barely breaking his stride in the moving column, let fall a single leaf of exercise-book paper bearing a simple crayon drawing of a racing car. Many of us had once been that boy. For a few hours, at least, some of us were again. And that, perhaps, was the biggest surprise and the most profound truth to be found in the death of Ayrton Senna. Those simple dreams, that unbought affection: maybe they justify it all.

Chapter Two

On a grey spring morning in the English Midlands the sleek little car smashed against the wall, its powder-blue bodywork exploding on impact, flying through the air in a shambles of torn fibreglass. A few seconds later the driver got out and limped to the pits. For an eleven-year-old boy, staring at the driver from behind a barrier a hundred yards away, it was a first glimpse of motor racing.

The perfectly mundane and unremarked crash of Sir John Whitmore, a wealthy amateur driver, in his Lotus Elite during a practice session at Mallory Park on Easter Monday 1959 took place at the very moment my father was shepherding my mother, my sister and me out of the field that served as a carpark, along a path between some bushes and into the trackside viewing area by the Esses, a curving double bend.

Here the racing cars flicked first to the right and then to the left in a single fluid movement. Leaving the Esses, the circuit climbed up a short straight to a right-handed hairpin, after which it doubled back to enter the finishing straight by means of a trickily cambered left-hand sweep known as Devil's Elbow. From where we were standing, if you looked across the Esses and the corner of the paddock, you could just see the tops of the cars skimming through. That was where Whitmore lost control and hit the wall. He got a shaking, nothing more.

And it was where, that afternoon, I watched with the beginnings of hero-worship as an unknown Scotsman named Jim Clark wrestled a huge and unwieldy Lister-Jaguar sports car to victories in three separate races. That made it four wins for Clark in the course of the afternoon, since he also won the race for which Whitmore had been practising, at the wheel of a second Lotus Elite.

Later in the day, after a picnic tea, we walked round the circuit and stood with a few hundred other spectators on a broad grass bank on the outside of Devil's Elbow. My sister and my mother weren't much interested by this time, but from there my father and I could see almost directly down into the cockpits of the cars, where bare forearms and string-backed gloves operated huge steering wheels with thin wooden rims and long slender gear-levers in a setting of dull aluminium and polished leather.

Clark, in his dark-blue helmet and leather-rimmed RAF surplus goggles, was clearly in a league above all the other drivers at this run-of-the-mill English club meeting. On every lap his arms worked back and forth as he fought the snub-nosed, bluff-tailed Lister down through the left-hand sweep, using the throttle to maintain the car's balance as the adverse camber did its best to throw him into the pit wall where the track straightened. The busy movements of his arms appeared to bear little direct relationship to the path of the car: the steering wheel would be spun in quick, deft jabs to the left and then to the right, but the car would maintain a curving trajectory as smooth as the howl of its six-cylinder engine.

Nobody had taught Clark, then a twenty-three-year-old lowland farmer, how to do this: it was just something he could do. An inbuilt sensitivity gave him the ability to drive the car beyond the normal limits of its roadholding, setting it up in what, in those days, was known as the four-wheel drift, by which the car was persuaded to take corners in long power-slides. To the spectator, even one who had never seen a motor race before, the result was the clear sight of a driver operating at the very limit of control, using the technique that had made heroes during the decade of men like Fangio and Moss.

For the next nine years I bought magazines, listened to the radio, and watched with mounting pride and pleasure as Clark ascended to absolute pre-eminence among grand prix drivers. Stirling Moss had been my first hero, indeed the embodiment of heroism in the immediate post-war years, but Clark came up with the generation of the sixties; he seemed more modern, closer to me. I saw him again during his career: at Mallory Park in 1962, winning the British Grand Prix at Silverstone in 1965, and leading the first lap of the 1967 Belgian Grand Prix at the wonderful old Spa-Francorchamps circuit. He had won two world championships when he was killed on 7 April 1968.

Men find beauty in racing cars; they stand and stare at them for hours. But the strange visual potency of the cars is not what draws 100,000 people to Silverstone for a grand prix. The emotional trigger is the sight of a driver visibly fighting the machine. It is what an eleven-year-old boy recognized that day in 1959 as he marvelled at the sight of Jim Clark wrestling the Lister-Jaguar down through Devil's Elbow. And it is what millions saw when they watched Ayrton Senna in a Formula One car in the years between 1984 and 1994.

In his ability to express a remarkable gift in terms that the ordinary fan could appreciate, Senna was just about unique. Other drivers have been fast and exciting: from Tazio Nuvolari in the thirties to Nigel Mansell in recent years, many have sent the pulse-rates rocketing in the grandstands through simple courage. The favourites were those accustomed to taking a car beyond its limits as a matter of course, trying to overcome the odds through sheer force of will. They could take an inferior machine and wring out the last drop of its speed, and the crowd could see it happening.

Other great drivers achieved their speed by a different method, avoiding drama in the belief that calmness and neatness were more likely to result in consistently good times. Fangio was like that, and Moss, usually, and Clark (despite his battle with the Lister-Jaguar, which turned out to have been an untypical display), and Stewart, and above all Alain Prost, whose brain was so calculating and devoid of a natural dramatic instinct that he was nicknamed 'The Professor', which is a funny thing for a racing driver to be called.

Ayrton Senna, perhaps uniquely, combined a smoothness of technique, a calculating brain and an unshakeable belief in his own superiority with a powerful aggression and a need to go as fast as possible all the time. And that, perhaps crucially, was where he differed from the only man with whom he truly bears comparison.

Chapter Three

When Senna's car hit the wall on the outside of Tamburello at 2.17 p.m. on 1 May 1994, bits flying off as it spun wildly back to the edge of the track, an old man a continent away switched his television off almost before the wreckage had come to rest.

'I knew he was dead,' Fangio said later.

Most people watching the TV coverage were still staring at the pictures, praying for Senna's safety. After the lurid televised accidents to Berger, Piquet and others in recent seasons, they knew that the evidence of the eyes could be contradicted by reality and that, given the strength of the modern grand prix car, it was possible for a driver to survive such a holocaust – especially at Tamburello. When Nelson Piquet stepped out of his wrecked Williams with only a bruised left leg and shaken wits after hitting the concrete wall backwards at full speed in practice for the 1987 race, and when Gerhard Berger escaped from the inferno of his blazing Ferrari at the same spot two years later with nothing much more serious than seared hands, it was clear that miracles could happen. But sitting at home in the town of Balcarce, where many years ago the people built a museum to commemorate the exploits of their most famous son, eighty-two-year-old Juan Manuel Fangio knew enough to see beyond the television pictures.

Of all the greatest champions of motor racing, the dozen or so who form the rank of the immortals, Fangio was perhaps the one whom Senna most closely resembled. For decades after his retirement, Fangio's total of five world championships between 1951 and 1957 was accepted as being beyond reach. Jack Brabham, Jackie Stewart, Niki Lauda and Nelson Piquet each won three, but never looked like challenging the great Argentinian's absolute pre-eminence. Even when Alain Prost won his fourth title, it was with the last gasp of his Formula One career, and a powerful following wind. Only Ayrton Senna could raise his eyes to what had seemed a target forever out of range. When he died, with a fourth title in his sights, he was only thirty-four years old; the 'Old Man', as Fangio had been known, had been forty-six when, as reigning champion, he pulled into the pits at the end of the 1958 French Grand Prix, unbuckled his helmet and called it a day. Almost forty years later, it is certainly true that the greater physical demands on drivers require them to be younger and fitter, and a forty-six-year-old world champion is virtually unimaginable. Still, thirty-four is nowhere near Formula One's retirement age. Senna was certainly no longer in the flush of youth when he died, but his performances throughout the preceding season left no doubt that he was still in his prime. Beyond question, there were world championships left for him to win.

Quite obviously he shared with Fangio such basic race-day attributes as a phenomenally refined driving technique, a high degree of mechanical sensitivity, an acute sense of racecraft and a willingness, *in extremis*, to abandon the finesse for which he was noted and call instead upon reserves of raw aggression. But beyond all that, the trait most obviously linking them was a political shrewdness placed in the service of a cold-eyed self-interest. Secure in the knowledge of their own virtuosity, both men recognized that it was worth nothing unless applied in partnership with the right vehicle: in other words, the car offering the greatest mechanical advantage at any given time. Like Senna, Fangio moved throughout his career from team to team, exploiting an uncanny ability to predict which was in the ascendant and which in decline, and never letting sentiment get in the way of his decisions.

After establishing his reputation with heavily modified American saloon cars in the marathon races that wound across Argentina, Bolivia and Peru during the 1940s, Fangio arrived in Europe in 1949 and, subsidized by President Juan Perón, began winning races in a Maserati entered by the Argentine Automobile Club. Noting his string of successes at San Remo, Pau, Marseilles, Albi, Perpignan and Monza, the all-conquering Alfa Romeo team invited him to complete their line-up by joining two illustrious veterans, Luigi Fagioli and Dr Giuseppe Farina, for the following season, the inaugural year of the world championship. Farina, whose relaxed style provided the model for the young Stirling Moss, won that first title, with Fangio as his runner-up; each had won three of the year's six Formula One races. Fangio won three more in 1951, the cerise Alfetta taking him to the first of his five championships. In 1952 and '53 the championship series was run to the specifications of Formula Two, and Fangio's Maserati was no match for the Ferrari of Alberto Ascari, who won nine grands prix in a row, setting a record which still stands. For 1954, however, Fangio was signed to lead the Mercedes-Benz team, making their post-war return to the tracks which they had dominated in the triumphalist heyday of National Socialism. The titles of 1954 and '55 were as good as won, and Fangio took the chequered flag in eight of the eleven races entered by the team over the two seasons.

When Mercedes withdrew from all racing after the Le Mans crash of 1955, in which one of their cars ploughed through a public enclosure killing eighty spectators, Fangio signed with Ferrari for 1956. He won the title in the last race of the season, at Monza, after his car had broken down, when the young Englishman Peter Collins forfeited his own chance of the title by voluntarily handing his Ferrari over to the team's number one. In those days a shared drive yielded half points, and the three points for half of a second place were enough to give Fangio a winning margin in the championship over Stirling Moss. Had Collins refused to give up the wheel, the full six points would have made him the first British world champion, at the age of twenty-four; he was to die two years later in a crash at the Nürburgring, before he could win the title that surely would have been his. Enzo Ferrari, the old schemer, had warmed to the blond, handsome, open-hearted Collins in a way he never could to Fangio, partly because of the Argentinian's more reserved nature but also because Ferrari knew he could never exert the degree of control over Fangio's destiny that he enjoyed wielding over the careers of the ambitious, vulnerable young Italians and Englishmen who otherwise made up his team. Fangio, already a triple champion, had in addition been responsible for many of Ferrari's worst defeats, and owed old Enzo no fealty or even undue respect.

Unlike the rest of the motor racing world, which first respected and later deified Ferrari, Fangio saw him for what he was: a small-town car builder with an incurable addiction to intrigue. For this perception, and the lack of the usual sycophancy that it engendered, Ferrari could not forgive him. 'A strange man, Fangio,' Ferrari wrote a few years later, in *My Terrible Joys*, a memoir in which he luxuriated in the treachery of others and in his own anguished rectitude. 'A great driver, but afflicted by persecution mania . . . I think it unlikely that we shall ever again see a champion capable of such sustained successes. But Fangio did not remain loyal to any team. He was conscious of his ability, he invariably used any means to ensure that he should if possible always drive the best car available at that moment. And he was successful in this, placing his self-interest – which was quite legitimate and natural – before the affection which has, instead, kept other great drivers faithful to a certain team through good and ill fortune.' Ferrari's hypocrisy took the breath away. This was a man who had seemed to take a malevolent glee in first hiring and then destabilizing driver after driver – Jean Behra, John Surtees, even Niki Lauda, who had won two championships for him after a long drought – and here he was levelling a charge of disloyalty at the greatest figure in the game, a man whose competitive instincts were forged from steel but whose sporting behaviour was entirely impeccable.

Fangio's speed seemed to derive from the very serenity of his temperament, yet his finest hour came on a day when he acted against his instincts, abandoning his suave control when brute vigour offered the only chance of a result. His lifelong maxim was that the best way to win a race was at the lowest possible speed, but his pursuit of the two young Englishmen, Peter Collins and Mike Hawthorn, at the Nürburgring in 1957 became perhaps the most celebrated act of sustained aggression in the sport's history.

The old Ring, laid down in the Eifel mountains near Cologne in the 1920s, provided the perfect theatre for such a god-like performance. Fourteen miles long, with more than 175 corners, including every variety of bend, surface and gradient, with hedges and ditches and spinneys to claim the unwise, it represented Formula One's last link with the original city-to-city marathons. The Ring's lap record, when the circus arrived for the 1957 German Grand Prix, was a shade over nine minutes and forty seconds; by the end of the race, Fangio was to have lowered that by twenty-three seconds. He had led in his cigar-shaped red Maserati from the beginning, but a bad pit stop put him almost a minute behind Ferrari's two English boys with ten of the twenty-two laps left. Driving with a kind of cold fury no one had seen him display before, Fangio, then aged forty-six, reduced the gap to nothing, overtaking Collins and Hawthorn, whose combined ages barely surpassed his own, in a shower of dust and pebbles as he slid by on the inside, using the ditches and the verges. All his virtuosity was on display that day.

Like Fangio, Senna was keen to adjust the odds in his favour whenever possible. Senna firmly believed he was the best, but he also knew that he was involved in a sport so devised that he could only prove his supremacy if the conditions were right, and that no effort to squeeze the last fraction of improvement out of those conditions would be wasted. Right from the beginning, he showed neither an inclination to accept simply what was on offer nor, if he was going to say yes, to take it in the form in which it was originally presented to him. He would go on demanding until he got what he wanted, and he didn't much mind whose finer feelings were disturbed while he did it. When Niki Lauda described him in 1985 – with only the evidence of Senna's novice year in Formula

One to go on – as 'probably the greatest talent to emerge in recent years', he added: 'By this, I don't just mean his fast lap times, but also the way he has come to grips with the whole business. He simply understands what is going on. I'm particularly impressed by the speed with which he has matured without making mistakes along the way.' But, again like Fangio, Senna's most glorious achievement came in a moment when he allowed passion to take over from cool calculation.

It happened at the 1993 European Grand Prix, a race added to the calendar at the last minute because of the cancellation of another event and awarded to Donington Park, a pre-war rendez-vous rebuilt and reactivated in the seventies through the enormous energy and financial commitment of a mutton-chopped Leices-tershire building contractor named Tom Wheatcroft. As a boy, before the war, Wheatcroft had watched the giant Mercedes and Auto Unions leaping over the bumps, the scream of their super-charged engines reflected off the brick walls of the farm buildings. It was his dream to bring Formula One back to the circuit which, though redesigned, widened and resurfaced with high-grip tarmac as smooth as a silk shirt, still contained within its undulating contours the beating heart of the old track. On 11 April 1993, Easter Sunday, his vision came to life as the cars formed up in front of the grandstands for the third round of the world championship. And Ayrton Senna gave him a race fit for his dreams.

Alain Prost and Williams had won the season's first grand prix, in South Africa, while Senna – second in that race but so dismayed by the decline in the performance of his McLaren that he had been contemplating a retreat into a sabbatical year – took the next round, in Brazil, by coping with the drizzly conditions better than anyone else. So, quite unexpectedly, Senna led the championship. At Donington, he intended to keep the initiative.

In the two days of practice, under a lowering sky but on a dry track, the Williams-Renaults of Prost and Damon Hill displayed the technical advantage which had made them the firmest of pre-season favourites. With a characteristic lack of visible drama, Prost recorded the fastest lap ever driven round the track, ahead of Hill, his willing dauphin, whose modest presence in the team had suited Prost's purposes rather better than the prospect of a challenge from Senna in an equal car. In fact it was Hill's performance rather than Prost's that gave the clue to the superiority of their cars: this was only the Englishman's fifth grand prix, and while he was clearly a competent professional racing driver, he had yet to convince experienced observers that he could compete with the élite. At thirty-two, Hill owed his seat in the team to his diligence as a test driver the previous season, and to the fact that he would not make trouble; but more than those considerations, to Prost's political skill in fighting off Senna's challenge. Third on the starting grid, more than a full second behind Hill, came Michael Schumacher, a fraction in front of Senna, whose McLaren was carrying a less powerful Ford engine than Schumacher's Benetton.

Senna may have been leading the championship, but no one was really giving him much of a chance at Donington. Only the possibility of rain undermined the certainty of a Williams walkover. In the dry, the power of the French engines plus the excellence of the Williams team's active suspension system and other computer-controlled driver aids would be enough to settle the race. But if it rained, Prost's well-known aversion to the wet and Hill's lack of self-confidence might become the determining factors. Still, Schumacher's outstandingly fast and confident performance in the rain to win his first grand prix at Spa the previous year suggested that under no conditions would Senna's task be straightforward.

It was an awful day: cold, grey and wet. Not at all the setting for the kind of glamour circus that Formula One's marketing men have tried to promote since television became its worldwide medium. And, in the April murk, fewer than 50,000 turned up at Donington: a third of a decent grand prix gate at Silverstone in high summer. Most fans had already booked their seats for July's British Grand Prix at the converted airfield fifty miles down the

M1, and were not anxious to double their investment in Formula One by finding another £60 or £70 a head for Donington. So Tom Wheatcroft, it was said, was financing this race to the tune of five million pounds.

The Princess of Wales and King Hussein of Jordan toured the pit lane on race morning, squired by Jackie Stewart. All of them tried hard to pretend that this was Monaco, but the anthracite skies of the afternoon looked down on blank spaces yawning in the mud-banks above the treacherous Old Hairpin, there were huge gaps in the grandstands facing the hairpin before the finishing straight, and entire blocks of seats were left vacant in the terraces above the spectacular Craner Curves.

The rain eased off just before the start, but the track surface was still soaking when the cars came out. Only one driver, J.J. Lehto in one of the all-black Saubers, took the chance of opting for ungrooved dry tyres – a gamble that had worked spectacularly well for his fellow Finn and mentor Keke Rosberg at Monaco ten years earlier, when Rosberg's Williams had simply jumped up and run away from a field of faster cars. No such luck this time: there was just too much water on the track. And there was Senna, hands and feet and brain working together as perhaps never before, at a pitch that made it seem as though this day was the consummation of all the thousands of hours of hard work and mental preparation he had given to the job since, as a poorly co-ordinated four-year-old, he sat in his first go-kart.

The red light turned to green, burning through the murk. Prost got off well, immediately assuming his station in front of Hill. Senna started poorly, and had dropped a place to fifth by the end of the short straight leading into the first corner, Redgate. He had been forced wide, over to the left of the track at the end of the pit wall, by Schumacher, who had been pushed off his own line by Karl Wendlinger in the other Sauber. His left-side tyres running off the track, Senna braked carefully, turned the wheel, and dived inside Schumacher going into the long right-hander. Biting at

Wendlinger's heels, clinging to the racing line, Senna held off Schumacher, who could not risk an attack using a part of the track that had not been even partially dried by the passage of the field during the parade laps.

Sweeping out of Redgate, heading downhill into the Craner Curves, Senna took his own big risk: looming in Wendlinger's mirrors, he chose to drive around the outside of the Austrian in a wide left-handed arc that took him on to the wettest part of the track. Wendlinger, knowing that this was only the first lap of a long race, and recognizing the yellow helmet in his mirrors, prudently chose to let Senna go, but not without a gasp of awe and admiration inside his own helmet as the red and white car floated around the tightening right-hander at the bottom of the curves and sprinted up the incline in pursuit of its next quarry.

Coming up behind Hill's Williams, the two cars throwing up thin streamers of fine spray, Senna positioned himself again to the inside as they approached the Old Hairpin, a right-hander. Here, close to the spot at which Tazio Nuvolari's Auto Union had hit and killed a stag in practice for the 1938 race, the Brazilian claimed another victim, with the sudden conclusiveness of his inside pass astonishing Hill, who lacked the wherewithal to resist. But the Englishman was then in the box seat to watch through the spray as Senna screamed down the back straight, preparing the next incident in this tumultuous mini-drama.

Prost, despite enjoying the advantage of being able to see where he was going, could do nothing to hold back Senna's advance. By the time they reached the Esses, the start of the circuit's final loop, the McLaren was on the tail of the leader's Williams. When they reached the Melbourne hairpin, a panoramic 180-degree job, Senna took the inside, again off the racing line, but delayed his braking long enough to gain possession of the corner. Both cars wavered and twitched, but only one gave in. It was Prost, who knew what the cost would be if he disputed Senna's right to take the corner. Senna knew that Prost knew. And knew that Prost would let him go.

Up above the pit in the press room, where correspondents follow the race on TV monitors, experienced people were looking at each other with awe in their eyes. History had just been made. In one minute and 35.843 seconds, Ayrton Senna had written another paragraph in the story of motor racing. Something, it seemed clear, to rank with Fangio at the Nürburgring. Which meant the greatest of all time.

In simple terms, it was a race decided first by that opening lap and then by Senna's mastery of pit-stop strategy in the changing conditions.

But it was not as straightforward as that. After twenty laps or so I left the press room and walked through the tunnel that leads under the grandstand and to the back leg of the circuit. There, from the vast empty spaces of the spectator terracing, I looked down on the majestic uphill sweeps, and saw grand prix racing as it was meant to be.

Vainly pursued by Hill, Barrichello and Prost (who got himself tied up in a sequence of seven botched pit stops that owed more to Jacques Tati than standard grand prix practice), Senna blasted majestically through the murk, plunging down through the curves and sweeping up the hill as Rudi Caracciola and Bernd Rosemeyer must have done in the thirties, no longer worried about what was happening to anybody else. He might as well have been all alone out there.

With Prost condemned to an afternoon of almost ritualistic humiliation, the conclusion was simple: Senna was profiting from a decade spent exploring the limits of physical and psychological domination within his sport. The Frenchman was not the only one to know how it felt.

Chapter Four

There is another Brazilian word that takes some explaining in English: *ginga*. The first g soft, the second hard, it defines a certain quality of grace in movement. In a woman, it is usually summoned to suggest a kind of sensuality. In a businessman, it can be a gift for tricky, perhaps devious, negotiation. It has to do with equilibrium, but also with originality and flair. A *capoeira* dancer, performing a sort of martial art with knives attached to his heels, needs plenty of *ginga*: nimbleness, balance, fluidity, continuity, a sort of arrogant courage.

There were Brazilian world champions in Formula One before Ayrton Senna, but he was the one who brought to it the quality of the *capoeira* dancer. Nigel Mansell and Alain Prost probably would not have put a name to it, but that was what they faced on numerous occasions when they raced head to head with Senna and came off worst – Mansell at Spa in 1987, Prost at Estoril in '88 and Suzuka in 1990, or Mansell again at Adelaide in '92.

These were incidents through which the very nature of grand prix racing was changed utterly, and probably for good; and since Senna was not only their common denominator but also their catalyst, we can say that he was responsible for this great and disturbing change – by which a sport which had always depended on the inherent chivalry of its participants suddenly came to accommodate the possibility of the systematic application of controlled violence.

All of these individual incidents are worth examination, but the one at Adelaide in 1992 was the last such of Senna's career. It was the final round of the season, with the championship already Mansell's, and the decision taken that the Englishman would be leaving for America at the end of the season, removed from his seat with the Williams team by Prost's subtle backstage manoeuvres. Mansell wanted to end his Formula One career and his championship season with a win, and he jumped straight into the lead, with Senna on his tail. But on lap nineteen something happened, and the McLaren went into the back of the Williams, both cars spinning off the track and out of the race. Mansell ran away from the scene, straight across the track towards the pits; afterwards he told reporters that he'd done it to stop himself punching Senna. 'All I know is that someone hit me up the back when I was turning into the corner,' Mansell said. 'It seems that certain people in Formula One can get away with anything. I didn't go near him afterwards because if I had there would have been a big fight and I don't think that's the right way to leave Formula One.' For his part, Senna claimed that Mansell knew he was close behind, but had braked early for no apparent reason.

Commentating for BBC television, James Hunt immediately took Mansell's side. 'Nigel Mansell is absolutely the innocent party,' the former world champion announced as the cameras lingered on the two ruined cars. Back home, Mansell's huge informal fan club rose up in fury against the wicked South American whose characteristic trickery had ended their man's chance of closing his grand prix career with another champagne shower.

But what else did they expect? It was, after all, just like Senna. Remember Spa, when he pushed Mansell off the track, and the burly Nigel grabbed the slight Senna by the throat in the pits afterwards, and had to be dragged away by three mechanics? Or Estoril, when Senna had made his car lunge across the track at Prost (his team mate, for goodness' sake) while they were both doing 190 m.p.h. in their McLarens down the main straight, right in front of the pits? Or Suzuka, where he rammed Prost from behind at 100-plus in the first corner, knowing the Frenchman had to win the race to keep alive his hope of the world title? So when Senna crunched his McLaren into the back of Mansell's Williams at Adelaide, it simply seemed like part of the Brazilian's established pattern of behaviour. The extension of this line of reasoning was a stab at guessing Senna's motivation. Perhaps he just wanted to deprive Mansell of the satisfaction of ending his world champion-ship season with a win. Perhaps he wanted to hoist a signal for the next season, one announcing that while he might have lost his title, he was nevertheless still not a man to trifle with.

But that's not how all Englishmen saw it. 'Mansell ran away because he knew it was his fault,' Dave Coyne said the next morn-ing. 'He'd given Senna a brake test. It's the kind of thing only another driver could see. The stewards wouldn't have a clue.'

Rick Morris agreed. 'Mansell braked early,' he said. 'Of course, in a situation like that it has to be the fault of the guy who's behind if he hits the guy in front. But at 170 miles an hour, if someone's that close behind and you lift your foot even a hair, there's noth-ing he can do. And if he hadn't been that close, he wouldn't have been Senna.'

Dave Coyne and Rick Morris are not household names in motor racing. What made them different from most other middle-aged Home Counties motor traders rewinding the video of the Austral-ian Grand Prix was that they had both raced against Ayrton Senna before the world knew about him. And each of them could fit the events of Adelaide into another, perhaps truer pattern of behaviour.

'I've had accidents with Senna,' Coyne said, remembering the 1981 season, when he and Morris competed with the Brazilian in the British Formula Ford championships. 'He was always aggres-sive. He had a very strong belief in himself. He believed he was the best. His life was a hundred per cent motor racing.'

At the time Coyne was twenty-three, hoping for a career as a top-line driver; Senna was twenty, and just out of go-karts. Morris, on the other hand, was thirty-four, a comparative veteran, and he remembered with special clarity an accident on the opening lap of a race at Oulton Park in Cheshire that year. 'I was on pole posi-tion, considerably the quickest in practice,' he said. 'At Oulton, you go up the hill and into a right-hander with a double apex. It's not one of the accepted passing places, and going into it on the first lap I thought I had a good lead when suddenly he came up and banged me out of the way. I got back on the track in tenth place. He won the race.' It was one of twelve wins in twenty starts for Senna that year, his maiden season in racing cars. As early as that, people were talking about his talent in a special tone of voice, but to some the incident with Morris and several others like it seemed to set the mould for his future behaviour. Senna, it appeared, thought he had a divine right to win, and woe betide anyone who got in his way; even when, like Mansell at Adelaide, his opponent had a faster car.

Right from the beginning, Senna had what they call natural speed, but the ability to drive a car round a circuit faster than anyone else isn't the hardest part of being a racing driver. What is more difficult is the bit that actually makes it racing as opposed to high-speed driving: the overtaking. And although Senna's sixty-five pole positions in 161 grands prix attested to his pure speed, the overtaking was what he was best at. Better, perhaps, than any man who ever sat behind the wheel of a racing car.

During successive seasons graduating through the junior single-seater categories – Ford 1600, Ford 2000 and Formula Three – other drivers quickly became accustomed to giving Senna room. When they didn't – as his Formula Three rival Martin Brundle refused to on several occasions during 1983 – they often ended up on the grass or in the sand trap. Nor did it take the world of Formula One long to get the idea. Right from the occasion of his début in a Toleman-Hart at Rio de Janeiro in 1984, Senna made it clear that he wasn't scared to hold the inside line of a corner against pressure from more experienced men. Once he had established himself as a front-runner, slicing past dozing backmarkers became a particularly emphatic component of his repertoire. Some slow men kept an eye on their mirrors, and knew to get out of the way when the yellow helmet showed up; when he came across one who wasn't paying attention, he showed an astonishing gift for getting by without wasting time. He never held back, and most of the time he brought his manoeuvres off. It was a form of psychological pressure: other drivers got used to moving over when they saw that helmet. Whether they would admit it to themselves or not, they had done half of his job for him. 'He took no prisoners,' Brundle was to say ten years after their Formula Three duels. 'He had that brightly coloured helmet, and you could clearly see him coming up behind you. He left you to decide whether or not you wanted to have an accident with him. What you did depended on how badly you wanted to finish the motor race.'

All this was to become most starkly evident during the course of the 1989 and 1990 seasons, when Alain Prost, his chief rival, was so emasculated by the Brazilian's superiority – no, not just by that superiority but by an unhesitating willingness to brandish it before the world's audience, a willingness that would have seemed sadistic had it not been self-evidently the product of his conception of destiny – that he seemed to lose the capacity to overtake not just Senna but anyone at all.

Motor racing, at whatever level, takes the competitive urge to an extreme further than any other sport. It might not dismantle a player's psyche in public in the naked and sometimes unbearably protracted way that a tennis match can do; it might not take him as far beyond his physical limits as a third consecutive day in the Alps during the Tour de France, when drugs become less of a method of gaining an unfair advantage than a necessity to deaden the pain; it might not require the mad courage of a downhill skier, who throws himself out of the start-hut and down a glass wall without any form of protection; barring accidents, it will certainly not hurt as much as any run-of-the-mill boxing match. More than any of these, however, motor racing, head to head and in hot blood, presents a test of manhood. Uniquely, the car becomes a weapon: encasing the driver, armour-plating him, it responds exactly to his bidding. Its capabilities are a direct reflection of his power – either his purchasing power, in the case of a road car, or the power of his talent and reputation, in the case of a Formula One car. Even after a century of motoring, and in an era when all sensible people recognize the internal combustion engine's threat to the environment, the car remains the clearest and most potent symbol of selfhood. And if such factors can lead the drivers of saloon cars in the morning rush hour to mad rage, with nothing at stake beyond momentary pride, it does not take much to imagine the degree of emotional intensity involved when the contest – the race – becomes the whole point of existence.

Usually these rivalries, whether momentary or long-term, are clear enough to the observer. But sometimes they are expressed in the form of hidden trials-within-trials whose existence is known only to the participants. Not even a James Hunt, with all his privileged insider's understanding of the men and the event, could be certain to spot it. Which is where Dave Coyne's 'brake test' came in.

The informal brake test is something you can see in its mundane form on an overcrowded motorway: two men in company cars travelling too close together in the fast lane, jousting, getting overheated, and the one in front dabs the brake pedal just to give the other a fright. At ninety on a public road it's stupid and dangerous; at 190 on a racetrack it sometimes becomes a tactic.

There are two reasons why a racing driver might use it. The first, a bit like the speedsters on the motorway, is to teach someone a lesson – usually a novice obstructing a faster man, who then cuts in front and gives his opponent a character-forming experience to ensure that he makes room next time. The second is less blatant but more profound in intention. In a fight between equals, what it may do is force the close pursuer to lift his own foot off the throttle in response, which unsettles the balance of his car. Executed in the run-up to a corner, before the accepted braking zone, it can make the second man lift, brake, accelerate and then brake again for the corner: four improvised decisions whose effect might cost the driver a vital length or two at a time when he could have been positioning himself to come out of the slipstream and overtake. Done with cunning, as Coyne suggested, it can be undetectable to the naked eye in the grandstands (or the stewards' observation window), its effect known only to the victim. Misjudged, it can at best give the pursuer a clear overtaking opportunity; at worst it can end with two cars tangling and spinning off the track.

Both Coyne and Morris mentioned it in connection with the incident between Senna and Mansell in Adelaide, and a voice from another era added his support to the view. 'The one thing Senna wanted to do was beat Mansell in Nigel's last race,' Stirling Moss said. 'The fact that he was so close shows how hard he was racing. But it's a business in which things can happen very fast. Maybe Nigel lifted off early. I don't know. Since that kind of accident must always be the fault of the man who was behind, I guess it was Senna's fault – but I don't think he was to blame, if you see what I mean.'

Why might Mansell have used it? To throw Senna off balance, perhaps. Or maybe he had braked early simply out of a sudden excess of caution, as Prost may have done when he threw the title away at Suzuka in 1990. More likely he was thinking back five months, to the Monaco Grand Prix. In this, a race Mansell had never won, the Englishman led by a comfortable half-minute until, with eight laps to go, a puncture brought him into the pits. There ensued a chase of brief but nevertheless epic proportions, culminating in a final lap throughout which the Williams, on fresh tyres, seemed to be trying to climb over the McLaren, which was getting no grip from its tired rubber. Somehow, against all probability even on a track notorious for making overtaking difficult, pitting his wits against a car that was probably three or four seconds a lap quicker at that point, Senna held Mansell off, to win by a length. And much later the vanquished driver explained, without rancour, how his rival had done it. 'Ayrton will sometimes slow up on a short straight just to make you back off,' he said. Looking at the video of that last lap, paying particular attention to the sequence around the swimming-pool complex, where the cars turn left, right, and left again before approaching the last corner, you can see, without the benefit of telemetry, that this is exactly what the McLaren is doing. 'Ayrton was perfectly entitled to do what he did,' Mansell said immediately after the race. But memories are long in motor racing, and the Englishman – who may have yielded nothing to Senna in terms of guts but never commanded anything like the same degree of tactical finesse – may just have been indulging an ill-judged and ultimately expensive desire to show the Brazilian that he hadn't forgotten that particular episode in their long and semi-private battle.

An alternative and rather more intellectually satisfying explanation came from another man who raced against Senna in the early days. Back in 1983, Davy Jones was an eighteen-year-old American prodigy competing for the British Formula Three title. At home in Nevada, between races for Jaguar in a US sports car series, he chuckled as he replayed the Adelaide video, remembering the time he sat back and watched as Senna and Brundle landed on top of each other at Oulton Park when the Brazilian tried a run down the inside and found the door locked. After paying the customary tribute to Senna's mental toughness, Jones said something very interesting: 'I wonder,' he said, 'if his thinking in a race isn't so far advanced that his mind is not relating to the incident that's actually happening. Maybe if Nigel lifted a bit early, Ayrton just wasn't prepared for it, because his mind was already two or three corners ahead. You know, when you take a corner, your mind goes to the turn-in, then to the apex, then the exit. You're always a step ahead of what you're actually doing. But maybe Senna is always three steps ahead. Maybe that was it. And maybe that's why he's such a great champion.'

But was that great champion responsible for bringing the hooligan tactics of Formula Ford to the more sophisticated and refined world of Formula One? Did he turn grand prix racing into a contact sport?

'It's not slot-car racing, after all,' Rick Morris said. 'It's not a non-contact sport. It's supposed to be a spectacle.' And he stated that he didn't think Senna was any more to blame for the changes in etiquette than Prost or Mansell or anybody else.

Stirling Moss agreed, but added that the term 'brake test' hadn't existed in his day; nor had the concept. 'If someone had tried it on me,' he said, 'I'd have gone and punched him in the face.' Davy Jones said wistfully that he wished he'd been racing in the sixties, against Moss and Jim Clark and Jackie Stewart: 'There's a lot of money involved now, and teams have to do well to justify and hang on to their sponsorship. That's certainly changed the ethics. Some of the moves you have to make now . . . well, in the old days they'd probably have taken a second thought.'

There was never a more contemplative grand prix driver than Ayrton Senna, nor one more obviously concerned with the philosophical questions raised by his occupation. Once he was in the car, however, he didn't go in for second thoughts; not about the dimension of his own talent, not about going for a pass at the first and slightest hint of an opportunity. He knew that this willingness to work in the margins was what gave him the advantage over those who were more inclined to pause, even for a microsecond, to check the odds and evaluate the risk.

Thinking back to the Formula Ford days, Dave Coyne got to the heart of it. 'I knew he was hard,' he said, 'and he knew I was hard. Once one of you gives way, it's all over. And once you have that edge, you've got to hold on to it.' Senna got it, and was in the very act of trying to hold on to it when he died.

Chapter Five

'Few people really know me,' he was to say in later years. And the rest, he added, the ones who thought they knew him but didn't, 'just don't understand what it takes from a racing driver who has dedicated all his life, since four years old . . . who has left family and friends behind, thousands and thousands of miles away, to live in Europe, and to go through all the steps to eventually come to Formula One . . . nothing has ever come to me easy.'

No doubt that's how he felt. To him, his entire career was a struggle. But the struggle was, quite literally, all in his mind. In terms of advantages, no aspiring world champion could have had more of a flying start.

He was born Ayrton Senna da Silva on 21 March 1960 in Santana, a northern suburb of São Paulo. The second child of Neyde Senna and her husband, Milton da Silva, he was two years younger than his sister, Viviane; a second son, Leonardo, was to follow. Milton, the owner of a successful metalworks specializing in the manufacture of car components, also bought a cattle ranch in Goiás in partnership with a friend; later the ranching side of the business extended to several farms, accommodating more than 10,000 head of cattle. In a country with many millions of very poor people and a small élite enjoying extreme wealth, it was a comfortable existence, and the legacy of a happy and secure childhood could be seen in the behaviour of the adult Ayrton Senna, to whom home, family and his native land remained the centre of life, a warm haven whenever his sporting and business commitments allowed.

There are two images which sum up the relationship of Milton and Neyde da Silva to the son they nicknamed 'Beco', and which perhaps explain much about his subsequent behaviour. The first is a photograph taken in the paddock at a go-kart meeting in 1973. It shows Milton and Ayrton looking proudly at the camera: the father has both arms around the son, in an embrace of fierce, protective pride, almost embarrassing to European eyes. The second is a fragment of film shot in the aftermath of one of Senna's pre-Formula One victories. Behind the pits at some English circuit, he and his mother fall into a triumphal embrace. As they begin to separate, his mother reaches up with her right hand and caresses her son's cheek as one would that of an infant. This was not a boy who ever went short of love, or of a belief in his own special place in the universe.

Attending first the Colégio Santana and later the select Colégio Rio Branco, he was given a general assessment of his work at the age of twelve. His overall grade was 68 per cent: decent, but not outstanding. By that age, however, he had already been driving for eight years.

He had been slow to walk, and at three was still having trouble co-ordinating the movements required to run or to climb stairs. His parents had taken him to a specialist, who examined an electroencephalogram and could find nothing wrong. Already, however, the boy had shown an interest in cars. At three, like most children, he had a pedal car, a little jeep; but when he was only a year older, by way of therapy, his father made him a miniature go-kart, a perfectly authentic device with a one-horsepower petrol engine from a lawnmower, a bucket seat and a smart front-fairing. Ayrton drove it in the grounds of the family homes. As soon as he was physically big enough he began driving a full-size jeep around the farm, making gear changes without using the old and practically worn-out clutch. It would not be stretching a point to call this the first recorded example of Senna's noted sensitivity to machinery, the more remarkable because no one had even taught him how to change gear with a clutch, never mind the more difficult art of clutchless shifting. He was then seven years old; before long he was being scolded for making unauthorized excursions on to the public roads.

Such tales are common among the biographies of the greatest

drivers. One hot afternoon in the late summer of 1904, the twelve-year-old Tazio Nuvolari, a farmer's son, took his Uncle Giuseppe's Bianchi out on to the road between Brescia and Ronchesana, mastering its controls without the benefit of instruction; automobiles immediately replaced unbroken colts in the boy's affections. At an even younger age Juan Manuel Fangio, one of six children born to an accordion-playing stonemason, was hanging around Señor Capettini's repair shop in Balcarce, fetching spanners for the mechanics; soon another garage-keeper allowed him to drive a wooden wagon powered by an old motorcycle engine, carrying the sweepings from the garage floor to the municipal dump. Maurice Trintignant was piloting a Bébé Peugeot around his father's vineyard in the Vaucluse at the age of nine. Stirling Moss, whose parents had both dabbled in motor sport, sat on his father's knee to take the steering wheel for the first time soon after his sixth birthday; five years later the father, a successful dentist, paid £15 for a 1929 Austin Seven which Moss learnt to throw around the fields of the family's farm. The boy Jim Clark also had the luxury of farmlands in which to learn the rudiments of controlling a four-wheel vehicle in unfavourable conditions. In Canada, near the St Lawrence River, the eleven-year-old Gilles Villeneuve drove an old pick-up truck round and round a field next to the old farmhouse bought by his father, a piano tuner. Nigel Mansell was twelve when he talked his father, an aerospace engineer who had raced go-karts, into getting him a kart of his own. Stockbroker's son Graham Hill, on the other hand, did not drive anything with four wheels on it until he was twenty-four, an apparent handicap which failed to prevent him from twice winning the world championship in the era of men as naturally gifted as Clark, Dan Gurney, Jackie Stewart and Jochen Rindt.

But Ayrton Senna, it is fairly safe to say, displayed a precocious natural talent as soon as he was physically able to express it. Nor does it seem that he had any other destiny in mind than the route, as straight and direct as possible, to the world championship. He began in go-karts, the nursery formula which established itself in the 1970s as the best way for young drivers to learn not merely how to handle a sensitive vehicle on a circuit at high speed but also how to race in close company with others.

He was encouraged by his father, who, like all his fellow countrymen, had taken pride in the growing achievements of Brazilian drivers in Europe, particularly those of Emerson Fittipaldi, another São Paulo boy, who in 1972 became his country's first world champion. Perhaps Milton da Silva's most crucial early intervention was to contact Lucio Pascual Gascon, nicknamed 'Tchê', an engine-tuner of Spanish origin whose horsepower had propelled Fittipaldi to his boyhood karting triumphs ten years earlier. Engine power was critical to the performance of the tiny karts; at Milton's request, Tchê cast an eye over the boy during a test session on the little kart track within the precincts of São Paulo's Interlagos circuit. 'If he carries on like that, he's going to win races,' the Spaniard told the father after watching a few laps. A deal was agreed whereby Tchê would build the boy's engines himself. The following Sunday, 1 July 1973, Ayrton was back at Interlagos to take part in his first race, and won. Soon he was spending all his out-of-school hours at Tchê's workshops, absorbing the basic elements of a knowledge that would make him technically the most formidable grand prix driver of his generation, fully able to converse with his race engineers in Formula One's own abstruse language of slip angles, spring rates and engine mapping.

His dedication was self-evident. 'Every time I went to the kart track he was there, training,' remembered Rubens Carpinelli, then president of the Brazilian national karting commission and later head of the São Paulo automobile federation. 'He was impressive. He was only a boy, ready to talk to anybody about his kart.' And, said Carpinelli, he was a loner, strong on self-reliance: 'His engines were prepared by Tchê, but he looked after all the rest himself. He was both the mechanic and the driver.' Even then, according to those around him, he entered a race with the sole object of winning. It was victory or nothing. And in pursuit of his goal he was already looking for perfection, attentive to the tiniest detail. His slight build helped: in a kart, even more than in a grand prix car, every kilo of the driver's weight and every square inch of frontal area have an impact on the performance of the vehicle, particularly at top speed in a straight line.

Two weeks after victory on his début, Senna won the junior category of the São Paulo winter championship. And when the summer season started, he fought his way to the full junior title. Already he was learning that no matter how talented you may be, the limits of your achievement are defined by the quality of your equipment; and the quality of that equipment is determined by your own ability to present yourself in the right place at the right time with the right qualifications and backing, and with the political skills necessary to ensure that you are the one who emerges from a crowded field.

The next year he won the national junior championship, followed in 1976 by the senior championship of São Paulo and victory in a big three-hour race in his new 100cc kart. This, too, was the season in which he first appeared in the yellow helmet with green and azure bands, painted to echo the colours of Brazil. The South American title fell to him the following year.

In 1978 he made his first racing trip outside South America, to enter the kart world championships at Le Mans. Milton contacted the Parilla brothers of Milan, Europe's top kart constructors, who arranged a test for the eighteen-year-old at the Parma-Pancrazio circuit in Emilia-Romagna. Their team leader, Terry Fullerton, also took part in the test session, supervised by Angelo and Achille Parilla. Fullerton, the 1973 world champion, was himself preparing for the races at Le Mans, but Senna attacked the unfamiliar track and ended the day outpacing him. The Parilla brothers signed him up as their second driver for Le Mans, and after a fortnight's preparation in Italy the team left for France, where they were joined by Tchê, dispatched at the Senna family's expense to give expert assistance with the team's engines. There Senna caused a minor sensation by qualifying in third place, and by finishing the race a scarcely less creditable sixth. He returned to Brazil, but a few weeks later travelled with the Parilla team to Japan, where he finished fourth at the Sugo circuit, the modest first step towards what would later become a profound mutual relationship with Japan's motor racing public.

He opened 1979 by finishing runner-up in the South American championship, in Argentina. A return to Europe saw him winning the San Marino Grand Prix and travelling to Portugal for the world championships, where he came second over a course laid out in the paddock area of the Estoril circuit.

He won his national championship again in 1980 and '81, but he never did manage to take the world title. Second again in 1980, mechanical problems lowered him to fourth and fourteenth in the subsequent years.

By the time of his last significant kart race, the Brazilian championship of 1983, his life had moved on. At nineteen, he had married Liliane Vasconcelos Souza, a childhood sweetheart from the same stratum of São Paulo society as the da Silvas, a girl with blonde hair and a figure that was still remembered years later as stopping traffic in the pit lane; and he had given up his studies at business school, which his father had hoped would provide the groundwork for his succession to the leadership of the family firm. He had decided instead – in fact he had made up his mind at the age of four and a half, according to his own later testimony – to become a racing driver.

After karts, the next stage would be a graduation to proper single-seater racing cars, and there was only one place to go for that. Since the sixties, England's club racing scene has represented the most effective finishing school for new talent from around the world, a battleground for young men who want to be world champion and need to prove their worth in a highly competitive environment.

The vitality of English racing has its roots in the work done in the 1950s and '60s by John Cooper and Colin Chapman, two icono-clastic engineers whose lightweight rear-engined Coopers and Lotuses were comparatively cheap to build and created an economic environment in which small-time racing could thrive. Unlike most of their predecessors in England, Italy, France and Germany, Chapman and Cooper decided not to build their own engines, but to buy them in. This simplified their operations, and significantly reduced the capital investment for men who were not subsidized by vast commercial empires. Their creativity revolutionized racing-car design around the world: Ferrari's Formula One cars look the way they do because of Cooper and Chapman, as do the machines that take the grid at the Indianapolis 500. Their legacy is not just in that achievement, or in the continuing success of the increasingly sophis-ticated partnerships between small, flexible teams such as McLaren and Williams and the major car manufacturers who supply their engines: Honda, Renault, Porsche, Ford, Peugeot and Mercedes-Benz. It is also to be found in the health and enduring importance of the various British single-seater series, a proving ground for inter-national talent from which the likes of Mika Hakkinen of Finland, Rubens Barrichello of Brazil, Damon Hill of England and David Coulthard of Scotland were still emerging in the nineties.

Ayrton Senna da Silva arrived in England in November 1980. With the support and guidance of Chico Serra, who was less than six months away from his own Formula One début, he headed straight for the headquarters of the Van Diemen company in Norfolk, where Serra introduced him to the company's founder, Ralph Firman. Confronting Firman was a slender, fine-featured youth with curly dark brown hair, a full-lipped mouth of the type usually described as sensual, soft mid-brown eyes (all inherited from his mother) and a reserved, self-contained manner that might have been shyness or might have been arrogance. Senna completed ten laps of the bumpy Snetterton circuit, a converted World War Two airfield, in a Van Diemen Formula Ford 1600. It was his first time in a proper single-seater racing car, and it wasn't an enjoyable experience: the car's handling didn't suit him, and there was no opportunity to make adjustments. But Firman, a former mechanic with a high reputation as a talent scout, had seen enough. Using Serra as a translator, since Senna at that point spoke little English, Firman signed him up for the forthcoming season, gently deflecting the novice's demand to be paid for the privilege in favour of a deal more closely reflecting the reality of their relationship, depending on a measure of subsidy from the driver's father.

Ayrton brought Liliane to England in the new year, and they settled into a rented flat near the Van Diemen factory in Norfolk. For Liliane, accustomed to a life of privilege at home in São Paulo, the realities of being a junior racing driver's wife in the English backwoods seem to have come as a shock. Nevertheless on 1 March 1981, after weeks of testing, Senna appeared on the starting grid for the first race of the season, in the kidney-shaped bowl of the Brands Hatch short circuit, entered under his full name alongside his two team mates, Enrique Mansilla of Argentina and Alfonso Toledano of Mexico. It was a good day for the team. Mansilla finished first and Toledano fourth, sandwiching two British drivers, Dave Coyne and Rick Morris. For Senna, his first car race was taking place on a circuit very different from the flat kart tracks of his previous experience: the first corner at Brands Hatch, called Paddock Bend, was a long and tricky right-hander, falling away into a wickedly vertiginous descent followed by a steep switchback up to a hairpin. He finished a respectable fifth, eight seconds behind the leader after twelve laps.

At Thruxton a week later he was third, beating Mansilla, his team leader, after a race-long battle. And one week after that, when the Formula Ford mini-circus returned to Brands Hatch, Van Diemen gave him a new car, and he won.

It rained for much of the day. The Brands bowl is a tricky place at the best of times; in the rain it can be diabolical, transforming already difficult corners like Paddock Bend and Clearways into skating rinks, while even the apparently harmless bits turn evil, thanks to small rivers that cross the track on the top and bottom straights. This was Senna's second visit to the place, in the third car race of his life, in an event contested by young men who all fancied themselves as future world champions. He beat Mansilla again in his heat, before walking away with the final by a margin of fifteen seconds.

It wasn't that Senna liked the English climate. He and Liliane both hated it, and early associates remember that he insisted on things like having his driving gloves warmed on a radiator. But rain, as it turned out, was something that he could work with.

Rain divides racing drivers like no other external factor. Sometimes those who may be lions in the sunshine, like the 1967 world champion Denny Hulme, men who would cheerfully race all day in a heatwave with their brakes shot to hell and petrol sloshing down their necks from a broken filler pipe, simply say no thanks at the sight of rain and settle for a comparatively easy day in midfield. This may be a sign of common sense rather than a want of courage. A man as hard as Niki Lauda once tossed away the chance of a world championship because he just didn't fancy the odds against survival in a downpour. Fear of the rain was a condition that would affect Senna's greatest rival; and to say that a refusal to take risks in the rain diminished the achievements of Alain Prost would be, in some eyes, to invite ridicule.

The real hero-drivers, however, have all used a wet track to demonstrate the qualities that set them apart, and that might add up to genius: Rudi Caracciola, Tazio Nuvolari, Stirling Moss, Jim Clark and Gilles Villeneuve among them. Rain exposes not merely outright courage but also a sensitivity of touch on throttle and brakes and steering, a way of doing essentially violent things in a gentle way. It also requires a perception beyond the normal limits of vision, in which shapes half-glimpsed through fountains of spray and heavy curtains of mist can be broken down by some mysterious super-rational process of interpretation into shape, speed, behaviour and likely intention, and instantly programmed into complex patterns of response and action. To anyone who happened to be tuned in to the events at Brands Hatch on 15 March 1981, Senna's maiden Formula Ford victory could be taken as a strong pre-echo of the wet-weather virtuosity to come at Monaco in 1984, when only an official's highly contentious decision to halt the race in a downpour robbed him of a win while he was serving his apprenticeship; in his first Formula One victory through the lakes of Estoril in 1985; and in that opening lap at Donington Park in 1993, a minute and a half of technique and commitment that came as close as anything could to summarizing an entire career.

The next race of his first season in England, at Mallory Park a week later, contained further important pointers to aspects of his future. His first pole position for the fastest lap in qualifying was another harbinger, this time of a hard statistic: sixty-five poles to come in 161 Formula One grands prix, including his last four races. Just as significant was the turbulent outcome of the race, decided on the last lap when Senna, in second place, attempted to go round the outside of Mansilla, the leader, on the exit from the big 180-degree corner at the back of the circuit. Mansilla held his line, pushed wide, and edged his junior team mate on to the grass, giving himself enough breathing space to hold on for victory. Afterwards in the paddock an exchange of verbal recriminations was followed by a scuffle which led to both drivers being restrained by those around them. Clearly, Senna felt injustice keenly. If he believed his rights had been infringed, he was prepared to take direct action.

There was another second place at Mallory two weeks later, the price of a tangle with his other team mate, Toledano, which permitted the canny Rick Morris to slip through in the later stages. But then, on a wet and blustery day at Snetterton, he again showed so well in the rain that the watching Dennis Rushen, manager of a successful Formula Ford 2000 team, walked up afterwards and made him an on-the-spot offer. He could do the 1982 British and European championships, Rushen said, for the bargain rate of £10,000. Senna thanked him, and filed the offer away.

Snetterton was the first of four consecutive wins, the sort of run which later characterized his domination of Formula One. Then at Silverstone in June he was beaten by Morris's dramatic leap over the kerbs at the Woodcote chicane in the last 300 yards of the race, a manoeuvre enshrined in club racing legend even before the cars were back from their lap of honour. In the next race, at Oulton Park, he dealt Morris a spectacularly abrupt form of summary justice, driving him off the track. At the same circuit in late July he began another streak, this time of six wins in a row, assuring himself of victories in both the RAC and Townsend Thoresen championships. The race that clinched the RAC title for the little black and yellow Van Diemen with the Brazilian flag on the cockpit cowling was another spectacular display in the rain at Snetterton. His record in his season in Formula Ford 1600 was twelve wins, five second places, one third, one fourth and one fifth from twenty starts.

But on his final podium appearance of the 1981 season, at Brands Hatch at the end of September, he announced his retirement. To general astonishment, he told the crowd in the post-race interview that he was not going to stay around for the Formula Ford Festival, an end-of-the-season weekend event that attracts 250 drivers, produces a single champion and has launched many important careers. Senna would have been the hot favourite. Instead he was going back to Brazil and giving up racing.

This seems to have been the only time he seriously contemplated relinquishing his vocation. The reasons were threefold: first, he wanted to see if he could satisfy his father's desire for him to prepare to take over the family's businesses. Second, he was a long way from home and was having difficulty enlisting support and, crucially, sponsorship, even though (with the aid of an English friend, the photographer Keith Sutton) he had been sending regular reports on his progress back to the media in Brazil. The third factor was the state of his marriage, disintegrating in the face of the pressures on Liliane, who neither understood nor enjoyed racing and found her unhappiness deepened by her husband's extraordinary intensity, the quality immediately noticed by everyone who met him.

When Senna returned to England early in 1982 to take up Dennis Rushen's offer, it was minus Liliane. 'I don't think of it as a mistake,' he later said of the marriage. 'I consider it to have been a very precious experience. We didn't have children, so no one else was hurt. We have both continued with our lives with no ill effects. It was simply that she wasn't made for me, nor I for her.' They were quietly divorced.

He also returned without any further obligation to follow his father into industry or farming. For four months he had tried to buck his destiny; now it was agreed that he should commit himself to following it. And with him came hard-won sponsorship from two Brazilian companies: Banerj, a bank, and Pool, makers of jeans, whose livery was to appear on his car, his overalls and his helmet for the next two seasons.

He held Rushen to the precise terms of his seemingly over-generous proposal. The team had been given Van Diemen's new cars to run on behalf of the factory, which for Senna meant pitching camp in Norfolk again, this time in a rented house with a fellow Brazilian driver, Mauricio Gugelmin, and his wife Stella.

The two-litre Formula Ford cars had slick tyres and wings, characteristics that brought them far closer to the behaviour of grand prix machinery and made them a much more complicated proposition, requiring greater attention to aerodynamic tuning. Senna arrived from Brazil too late to test the new cars, yet in his first race, again at Brands Hatch, he took pole position and won by fourteen seconds. Over the next five weeks he recorded five more poles and five more victories in a row; by the end of the season he had achieved twenty-one wins in twenty-seven starts, giving him both the British and the European championships.

Snetterton was among the more memorable of the year's victories. After losing ground as the result of someone else's accident he fell back to seventh, lost his front brakes (their lines cut by debris from the crash), yet clawed his way back to the front and won the race using only the brakes on his rear wheels.

The European championship took him to some of the circuits used by the Formula One championship, and at Hockenheim, Zolder and the Österreichring, the Formula Ford 2000s even acted as a supporting attraction to the grand prix meeting. It was at Zolder, in Belgium, that Senna tried to introduce himself to another fellow Brazilian, Nelson Piquet, the reigning world champion. But Piquet, a native of Rio de Janeiro and an expert in the art of relaxation, ignored the intense, unknown young *Paulista*. Perhaps it was not, after all, the best weekend at which to make such an approach: in qualifying, Gilles Villeneuve had killed himself by driving his Ferrari at full speed into the back of Jochen Mass's March, which was cruising back to the pits. The French-Canadian was an erratic genius beloved by the crowds; although his death did not seem as unbelievable as had Clark's and as would Senna's, it affected the world of Formula One deeply. But Piquet's snub was neither forgotten nor forgiven, and it continued to stain the relationship between them when Senna joined Piquet in Formula One two years later, going on to match his three world titles and far surpass his reputation. By that time, all Piquet's casual insults could not disguise his jealousy of the 'São Paulo taxi driver', for whom the full expression of his supreme gifts could be attained only through long and painful struggle.

In Austria three months later, another Brazilian did him an important favour. This time it was a fellow São Paulo boy, one who had known about Senna for years – indeed, had watched him emulate his own feats in the local and national go-kart championships. Emerson Fittipaldi had taken his two world titles into retirement, and had also shut down the team bearing his own name at the end of the previous season. But he was still on the scene, and at the Österreichring he took the opportunity to present his young compatriot to a number of senior figures. 'I introduced him to the major team managers,' Fittipaldi remembered. 'Ken Tyrrell, Ron Dennis, all of them. I had not done this with any Brazilian driver before.' Here, Fittipaldi told the elders of Formula One, was a driver who had everything it took to be a world champion. The subject of his testimonial stood by, looking embarrassed; but the big men, knowing Fittipaldi for a straight-talker, listened.

More sophisticated machinery was bringing the particulars of Senna's talent into focus. Those who experienced his driving on the public roads had ruefully commented on his way of going into corners and roundabouts at the highest possible speed, relying on his reflexes to handle the consequences. This was a habit that he carried with him on to the track, and it flew in the face of decades of conventional wisdom. In slow, out fast: that was the maxim for taking corners in a racing car for everyone from Fangio to Prost. Enter a corner too fast and you would waste time trying to stay on the road. Brake in good time, balance the car, floor the throttle as early as possible after the apex, get the power to the tyres without wasteful wheel spin or sliding: that was the way to win. In the era of aerodynamically induced downforce, making the old four-wheel drift obsolete, it became even more mandatory. But Senna was a racer, first and last, and modern racing, with wide cars on tight artificial circuits, is almost all done in the overtaking zone, which means the braking area before a corner. A driver who brakes early and neatly reduces his scope for overtaking, and therefore the possibility of racing. Who brakes last, and then manages to cope with the corner, wins. So Senna concentrated on refining his mastery of late braking, learning to handle the next phase – the 'turn-in' to a corner – with a unique combination of delicacy and aggression. Going for the fastest time in practice at a grand prix, Senna would make the car dart and shimmy on the entry to a corner, every twitch expressing the partnership of driver and car finding the limit of speed and adhesion. This was what John Watson, the distinguished Ulsterman, meant when he spoke, as he often has, of watching Senna overtake him and disappear on a hot lap during qualifying for the 1985 European Grand Prix at Brands Hatch, the only Formula One race in which they competed together. 'Senna's car was . . . dancing,' he said. 'Like raindrops on a pavement. The control . . . here was a driver doing things I had never even thought of, never mind attempted.'

Also apparent by this stage was Senna's disconcerting ability to start a race, psychologically speaking, in top gear. Most drivers require a lap or two to play themselves in, to feel out the conditions and the state of their car, and to get their tyres up to the temperature at which they begin to provide optimum grip – an absolutely vital factor in the car's potential lap speed. Not Senna, who worked out that this was the time during which, if he screwed himself right up, he could jump away, open a gap and establish an advantage that might not otherwise be available, given a parity of mechanical equipment. To do this takes not just skill and desire but unshakeable nerve and total commitment in the face of the unknown. It also requires the kind of sensitivity that can make a car go almost as quickly on cold tyres as on properly heated ones.

His other trick was to leave things late, so late that nobody else had time to do anything about it. The ability to summon speed to order lay behind his capacity for leaving his fastest qualifying lap until the last five minutes of practice, waiting until his rivals had set their times before going out and shattering their morale, condemning them to a night of scratching their heads and fiddling about with screwdrivers and software in an effort to get back on terms.

Midway through his second season in single-seaters, Senna was already receiving inquiries from grand prix teams. He and Keith Sutton had embarked on the unusual course of sending their weekly press releases to the Formula One team bosses, supplementing the intelligence that such men as Ken Tyrrell, Frank Williams, Peter Warr of Lotus and Ron Dennis of McLaren would be picking up from a weekly scan of *Autosport* and *Motoring News*. Alex Hawkridge of the small Toleman team was the first to show an explicit interest, offering Senna sponsorship for a season in Formula Three in exchange for his signature on an option for Formula One in 1984. Senna declined, indicating that although Formula Three was the next step, it would be taken on his own terms and with no hostages to fortune. Formula Three, like every other stage he had been through, would be entered with the best equipment he could get hold of, and no compromises. His extraordinary confidence allowed him to keep his options open, to turn down anything that might limit his room for manoeuvre or commit him to something less than the best available future.

He tried a Formula Three car twice in 1982. The first outing came during the summer when Eddie Jordan, then a fledgling team owner but already a talent scout of proven perspicacity, called to invite him to a day's testing at Silverstone, where after a few laps Senna managed to suggest a few small adjustments which subsequently carried Jordan's regular number one, the Englishman James Weaver, to a string of victories. Then, in November, he took part in an end-of-season non-championship race at Brands Hatch, borrowing the Ralt-Toyota which Enrique Mansilla, his team mate of the previous season, had been driving for the West Surrey Racing team with some success. According to the team principal, Dick Bennetts, Senna reasoned that if Mansilla had been winning races in the West Surrey car, then he would be able to do even better, because the results of the previous season had told him he was a more talented driver than the Argentinian. Senna took pole position, beat the lap record, and won the race by thirteen seconds. In January he signed with Bennetts, taking his sponsors with him.

Contrary to his habit, Senna did not claim pole position for his first race in the 1983 British Formula Three championship, at Silverstone. He lined up alongside a British driver, David Leslie, who had set the fastest qualifying time. But Senna was in the lead by the time they reached Copse Corner, the first bend, and won the race by thirteen seconds.

It was the first of nine consecutive victories, achieved under increasing pressure from a similar Ralt-Toyota in the hands of Eddie Jordan's protégé, the Norfolk driver Martin Brundle. Then aged twenty-three, nine months older than Senna, Brundle would have walked away with the championship had the Brazilian not been there. As it was, he failed to profit from a fire extinguisher going off in his rival's car at Silverstone (after Senna had overtaken him around the outside at the ultra-fast Stowe Corner) and from a missed gear at the start at Thruxton, while a downpour at Brands Hatch merely allowed Senna to display his precocious mastery of a wet track. Brundle had to wait until the tenth race of the season, the first round of the European championship at Silverstone, before he could profit from a series of spins caused by the Brazilian's poor choice of tyres. A week later Senna crashed in practice at Cadwell Park, writing off the car, putting himself out of the race and handing a second victory to Brundle. In the next race, at Snetterton, Senna chased Brundle so hard that they clashed on the penultimate lap when the Englishman closed the door, claiming the racing line as Senna tried to force his way through on the inside and went flying backwards into the barrier. Senna's heated protest to the clerk of the course cut no ice in the face of verbal testimony from the spectators at Brundle's home track.

Senna reasserted his supremacy at Silverstone, but then wobbled at Donington, where Brundle beat him fair and square by less than half a second – although the West Surrey camp were by now convinced that Brundle was getting more powerful engines from the Italian tuning shop which serviced both teams. Hostilities resumed at Oulton Park, where Brundle led until Senna tried a wild charge up the inside late in the race and took them both off. Senna defended himself to the stewards, but he was fined and his competition licence endorsed. Returning to Silverstone, he beat Brundle into second place but then found his suspicions of a British conspiracy confirmed when Brundle was allowed to keep his points despite an infringement of the technical rules – post-race scrutineering revealed that his sidepod was mounted one millimetre too low, a tiny discrepancy but nevertheless an illegality.

The lingering sense of injustice may have come into play at Oulton in mid-September, when Senna went off trying to take Brundle around the outside again. 'It appears he can't accept finishing second,' Brundle said, pointing out that a string of second places in the remaining rounds would still give Senna the title. He did not even manage that at Thruxton, his engine blowing up while he and Brundle were engaged in a dogfight. He avoided trouble at Silverstone, settling for second place under Brundle's rear wing, and wrapped up the title by winning at Thruxton in the final round, having driven to Italy and back to supervise the rebuilding of his engine to a specification matching that of Brundle's. Here Senna also took the risk of trying to warm up the engine more quickly by taping up the oil radiator; late in the race, with the temperature climbing dangerously, he found himself having to unbuckle his safety harness and lean out of the cockpit to remove the tape, a piece of spontaneous ingenuity more reminiscent of Nuvolari and the thirties than the high-tech world of contemporary racing.

It had been an enthralling championship, and one that provided the impetus for a pair of grand prix careers, but despite the occasional sign of vulnerability under pressure it was obvious which of the two drivers was going to do pretty well in a Formula One car, and which was a potential world champion. Davy Jones, then only eighteen years old, was one of the few men able to mount any sort of challenge to the two leaders during the course of the year. 'Senna was four or five years older,' the American said, 'and I felt he was already mature as far as being able to hold his concentration throughout a race. He didn't make mistakes. He was very quick wherever we went, and he was able to maintain a constant pattern. It was up to Martin Brundle and myself to try and match his pace.'

Jones also remembered how Senna raised the standard of

performance for the whole field, or at least those members of it capable of learning from him. 'Here's an example,' Jones recalled. 'At Silverstone in '83, going down the long back straight and down to Stowe, we were changing down to fourth gear, taking it flat.' ('Flat' in this context being driver-talk for having the foot hard down on the throttle.) 'Senna was much quicker. He was flat in fifth. It made the rest of us go from what we were comfortable with to flat in the next gear up.'

Nowadays, Jones observed, the cars work better the faster they go, thanks to developments in aerodynamics. 'You have to keep your foot on it. It's a confidence thing.' Senna was the one with the confidence not just to know that, but to exploit it. And, Jones added, 'He was very, very tough. He would do anything he had to do to make his car as wide as possible. If you did challenge him, it was up to you to make sure of a clean pass.' He remembered watching the Oulton Park incident in which the Ralts of Senna and Brundle ended up in a heap. 'It was so competitive . . . you drove with your mirrors as much as anything. Basically, it was blocking. And it's the same in Formula One. You don't make it easy for someone to get by. I didn't think Senna could settle for anything other than being in front. Mind you, I think all racers feel the same way. He's going to try to get by, no matter what it takes. Some of it was a little uncalled for, I guess.'

Jones also echoed the personal views of many drivers who raced against the Brazilian in his first three seasons in England: 'He was quiet, he kept himself to himself.' Senna's English was improving, thanks to lengthy technical conversations with Bennetts and his mechanics, but he seldom put himself out to open a conversation with his rivals, preferring to fill spare paddock hours playing with one of his collection of radio-controlled model aeroplanes.

It was as if even the mildest level of friendship with a competitor would add something that might get in the way when they were fighting hand to hand. As he was to prove in more exalted circumstances, he could be quite capable of showing his generosity towards another driver – but only when that driver no longer represented any sort of a threat.

Between the last two rounds of the British championship, Senna had travelled to Macau for the Formula Three race run through the streets of the former Portuguese colony. A Far Eastern replica of the race around the houses of Monaco, the Macau Grand Prix offered not just unusually good starting and prize money, de luxe accommodation and many parties, but also precious exposure to the attention of the Formula One bosses.

When Senna claimed pole position, saw off an early challenge from Roberto Guerrero, a Colombian driver already in his second season on the grand prix scene, and won the race – his first on a street circuit, a very different discipline from the wide open spaces of the converted aerodromes of English club racing – with ease, he was saying: I'm here. And his message was heard.

Chapter Six

There is a framed photograph of Ayrton Senna on the desk of Frank Williams's office in the modern factory building that stands in the looming shadow of Didcot power station. Senna died in his third race for Williams, in a car that left this factory in one of the huge blue and white transporters parked outside. But the driver and the team principal had been friends for more than ten years.

In 1983, during his year with Dick Bennetts in Formula Three, Senna had a home near Reading. Williams, who lived only a few miles away, invited him round to dinner two or three times, offering his thoughts and advice for the future. With the 1982 world champion, Keke Rosberg, and the popular Jacques Laffite committed to his team for that year and the next, Williams had nothing specific to put before the young Brazilian; for all their success, the team was not yet well enough established to justify such a risk. But Frank Williams loves motor racing with an intensity that few can match, and although he is notoriously parsimonious with drivers' salaries (a legacy of his early days of scuffling at the back of the grid, watching the pennies), he has always enjoyed encouraging young driving talent. That July, he became the first man to invite Ayrton Senna to drive a Formula One car.

Covering seventy laps in a day's testing at Donington Park, Senna took things steadily but nevertheless impressed the team by his speed and confidence in a car more than twice as powerful as anything he had driven before. The subtext of Williams's gesture was a feeling that although no partnership was immediately possible, perhaps in years to come Senna would not forget which of the big-time teams had first extended the hand of friendship.

McLaren were the next. Enduring a mediocre season with Ford

engines and two veteran drivers, Niki Lauda and John Watson, the team had just suffered the humiliation of failing to qualify either car for the Monaco Grand Prix, a severe blow to their fastidious principal, Ron Dennis. Approvingly described by Lauda as 'a manager with courage and ideas', Dennis was planning to drop Watson, hoping to attract Alain Prost from Renault as a partner for Lauda in 1984. But he was also on the lookout for fresh talent, since Lauda himself was planning only one more season. McLaren had big plans on the technical front: the new car would be designed by John Barnard, one of Dennis's partners, already famous for his unorthodox ideas, and powered by new Porsche turbo engines financed by another partner, the businessman Mansour Ojjeh, son of the boss of TAG (*Technique d'Avant Garde*), a Franco-Saudi high-tech engineering company. In his search for a junior driver, Dennis arranged a sort of beauty contest: a test day at Silverstone, during which he could compare the talents of Senna, Brundle and Stefan Bellof, a very fast young German making an impression in Formula Two. Watson, ironically enough, was asked to take the McLaren out first, making small adjustments to set it up and recording a target time against which the young hopefuls could be judged.

In the cold-eyed opinion of Formula One insiders, who quickly got to hear about it, Senna's behaviour that day went a long way towards establishing his absolute commitment to success. Of the trio, he went first. And went fast, quickly getting under Watson's time. On his fastest lap, however, the engine blew up. Back at the pits, he asked Dennis what his lap time had been. In Brundle's recollection, Dennis informed the young man that he was not inclined to think about pressing the button on a stopwatch when one of his cars was going past him with highly expensive smoke pouring out of the back. Once a new engine had been fitted, Brundle and Bellof took their turns, recording similarly impressive times. But then, to their astonishment, Senna buckled up his helmet, pulled on his gloves and went out for another session. While they were out having a go, he had been working on persuading Dennis that he should be allowed to run another few laps, on the grounds that Dennis's car had let him down the first time. Impressed by his persistence, Dennis sent him out, to be rewarded by the fastest times of the day – not surprisingly, since Senna had been given more of a chance to become acquainted with the car – and a matched pair of old-fashioned looks from the Englishman and the German, whose thunder had been stolen. An offer from McLaren duly arrived; but since it did not contain the guarantees Senna wanted, requiring him to spend another season in one of the lower formulas (subsidized by McLaren), before stepping up to Formula One, he had no hesitation in turning it down.

An interested observer at Silverstone on the day of the McLaren test – a spy, in effect, since he remained incognito at the back of the circuit – was Herbie Blash, manager of the Brabham outfit on behalf of its then owner, Bernie Ecclestone. On the face of it, Brabham were in much better shape than McLaren. Using BMW's enormously powerful four-cylinder engine and a secret petrol mixture enviously described by rivals as 'rocket fuel', the team was carrying Nelson Piquet towards his second championship title, with Riccardo Patrese in support. Seeing Senna as a likelier prospect than Patrese, whose talent seemed to have reached a plateau, Ecclestone invited him to a test on the high-speed circuit built by the French *pastis* millionaire Paul Ricard at Le Castellet, in the hills of Provence. This was Senna's first opportunity to try a turbocharged Formula One car. Revelling in its power, he demonstrated his gifts in the dart-shaped Brabham as successfully as he had in the obsolescent non-turbo Williams and McLaren, but when Ecclestone subsequently tried to make him a firm offer it was blocked by Piquet, who exercised a veto strengthened by his relationship with the team's main sponsor, the Italian dairy company Parmalat. Piquet didn't want Senna: not another Brazilian, not a *Paulista* and especially not one who might turn out to be as fast as himself, or even faster.

Senna bit his lip and listened instead to overtures from the Lotus team, recovering from the death the previous year of its founder and presiding genius, Colin Chapman. Peter Warr, Chapman's former right-hand man, had assumed control, and wanted to put Senna alongside Elio De Angelis, the team leader, replacing Nigel Mansell, who was thought to be a bit of a tiresome chap and anyway not very promising. But again the sponsors were to have their say. At Brands Hatch in late September Mansell put his car on the second row of the grid for the European Grand Prix, stealing the headlines in the British morning papers from De Angelis, who had qualified fastest. Lotus's sponsors, the makers of John Player Special cigarettes, saw the value of a successful Englishman to their marketing effort, and insisted that Mansell be retained.

His options closing down fast despite the admiration of practically every good judge in Formula One, Senna started paying serious attention to persistent advances from the small but ambitious outfit run by Ted Toleman, an English trucking magnate who had taken the plunge into Formula One in 1982 with a car powered by Brian Hart's turbo engine and driven by Derek Warwick. They had done well, for a brand-new team, but not well enough for Warwick, who announced his intention to join Renault, where he felt there would be a better chance of challenging for the championship. Faced with rebuilding a team on limited resources, Toleman's team manager, Alex Hawkridge, was confronted by two possibilities: to opt for an experienced driver on the way down, or to take a chance on the potential of a rising star. For his second driver, he chose Johnny Cecotto, a Venezuelan who had been a teenage prodigy in motorcycle racing in the seventies and still enjoyed a big following in Italy, the country of Toleman's chief sponsors. For his team leader, Hawkridge was keen to gamble on the rich promise of Ayrton Senna. And when Senna tested a Toleman-Hart at Silverstone, it took only two flying laps for the Brazilian to improve the best time ever set by a Toleman at the circuit.

Hawkridge made him an offer. Not a bad one, either: something like five times the money Brabham had proposed. But a Formula

One driver's market value depends on many factors. His own inherent ability is only one of them. The standing of the team ranged on the other side of the bargaining table is another. At any given time, only two or three drivers will be able to command the very top money from one of the élite teams. For the remainder, their reward will be assessed according to a shifting equation determined more by need than anything else: a driver's need for a particular car, a team's need for a particular combination of driving talent and sponsor-friendliness. Or, in either case, simply a need for money. And driving a Toleman was less likely to increase Senna's earning power, in terms of winning championship points, than a Brabham. But Toleman, on the way up and struggling for every foothold, needed him five times more urgently than the well-established Brabham, and would perhaps work five times as hard for him.

Senna signed a three-year deal, but not until he had got something he wanted even more than the salary: a special get-out clause giving him the right to leave the team and go elsewhere at any time if he was unhappy with the equipment provided, as long as he paid Toleman a specified sum of money before he made contact with other teams. During the negotiations, Senna made it clear that this arrangement, which was haggled over long and hard, was vital to him; he would sooner leave motor racing altogether, he told Hawkridge, than see his destiny slip away while he struggled on with a hopelessly uncompetitive car. Hawkridge saw his point; he had to, otherwise he would have lost his man.

When he arrived on the starting grid at the Jacarepaguá circuit in Rio de Janeiro on 25 March 1984, for the first round of the new season, he became the thirteenth Brazilian driver to compete in the world championship, two of whom had already claimed the title.

In the early post-war years, the most prominent South American drivers came from Argentina: the omnipotent Fangio was swiftly followed by José Froilan Gonzalez, Onofre Marimon, Roberto

Mieres and Carlos Menditeguy. Chico Landi was the first Brazilian, making his début in a Ferrari at Monza in 1951; over the next four seasons he raced Maseratis in five further grands prix, achieving nothing more than a lucky fourth place in an attritional race at Buenos Aires in 1956, at the age of forty-nine. History has little to say about Landi and even less about the next Brazilian, Gino Bianco, who raced a Maserati at four events in 1952 without scoring a point. Hernando 'Nano' da Silva Ramos was a figure of more substance, a Franco-Brazilian who raced Amedée Gordini's delicate little pale blue sports cars in the mid fifties and appeared seven times in Gordini's agile but underpowered Formula One machines in 1955–6, registering two points for a fifth place at Monaco in the latter year behind Moss, Collins, Behra and Fangio. The twenty-one-year-old Fritz d'Orey raced three times in 1959 at the wheel of an outdated Maserati entered by Scuderia Centro Sud, a private Italian team; two years later he was dead.

But then, in 1970, the year Brazil won its third World Cup with Pelé, Jairzinho, and the rest of the greatest soccer team ever assembled, came the man who established Brazil as a serious motor racing nation. From the moment Emerson Fittipaldi, only twenty-three years old, slid into Colin Chapman's sleek, low-line Lotus 72, he looked like a champion; two years later he became the youngest ever winner of the title. In 1974 he took his second championship at the wheel of a Marlboro McLaren. After one more season at McLaren, still at the height of his powers, he joined the team launched the previous year by his older brother, Wilson. But the cars, initially sponsored by and named after the Brazilian sugar company Copersucar, were never a match for his talent: ninth was his best championship position in those wasted years, and in 1980 he said goodbye to Formula One (although later in the decade he made an enormously successful comeback in American racing, winning both the Indianapolis 500 and the Indycar series championship). Wilson Fittipaldi never had his brother's flair, a fifth and a sixth place being the only distinguishing features of his two seasons with Brabham, while in 1975 he struggled to develop the initial Copersucar before retiring to make way for Emerson.

José Carlos Pace, nicknamed 'Moco', could well have become São Paulo's second world champion. He made his début in 1972, but one victory – in the Brazilian Grand Prix of 1975, five seconds ahead of Emerson Fittipaldi – plus three second places and two thirds were an inappropriate return for three highly competitive seasons with the Brabham team, whose ambitious owner, Bernie Ecclestone, became a close friend and was devastated when, early in the 1977 season, Pace was killed in a flying accident, aged thirty-two.

Luis Pereira Bueno, who had spent a season in England racing Formula Ford cars in 1969, qualified last and finished last at the wheel of an old Surtees in the 1973 Brazilian Grand Prix at Inter-lagos, during the first championship event held at the circuit. He and Ingo Hoffman, who made three appearances in the Fittipaldis' Copersucar in 1976 and '77, added nothing to the roll of honour. Nor, during the same years, did Alex Dias Ribeiro, a wild graduate from European Formula Two (where the nosecone of his car bore the legend 'Jesus Saves'), who paid for his ten races in a March but was frequently to be found in the list of non-qualifiers. Chico Serra, who introduced Senna to European racing, appeared at the wheel of Fittipaldi and Arrows cars in the early eighties, without making a lasting impression.

Emerson Fittipaldi's heir turned out to be Nelson Piquet, who arrived in 1978 at the age of twenty-five to take the wheel of an Ensign for what would be the first of more than 200 grands prix. Piquet's natural talent was so obvious that by the end of the season he had been transferred from the humble surroundings of the little Ensign team, first to McLaren and then to Brabham, where he stayed for the next seven seasons and the world championships of 1981 and '83. His third and final title, in 1987, came during one of his two seasons with Williams; after that his Formula One career wound down with a couple of seasons each at Lotus and Benetton before he moved to America, where a bad crash in an Indycar resulted in leg injuries that finished his racing.

When Senna arrived, then, Brazilians were a force in the Formula One world. They were known to have talent and money, although both commodities were not always present in the same package. (Argentina, by contrast, had long been eclipsed, only the gifted but moody Carlos Reutemann flying the blue and white flag after the fifties.) Nor were the Brazilian drivers subjected, as their footballers had so long been, to categorization according to the clichés of national temperament: the smooth style and cool calculation of an Emerson Fittipaldi bore little resemblance to the mercurial flair and improvised personal life of a Nelson Piquet. And Senna, too, presented his own personality to Formula One.

At Jacarepaguá he qualified on the eighth row of the grid – two thirds of the way down the field – in a Toleman left over from the previous year, but in the race he retired after only eight laps with a turbocharger problem. The same thing spoiled his run two weeks later in South Africa; nevertheless he finished sixth, three laps behind the winner, scoring his first championship point in only his second race. There was another point for him in the first European race, at Zolder, where he qualified nineteenth but lugged the old car round to the finish.

By this time the new Toleman was finished and ready back at the factory, but the team were delaying its appearance until the resolution of a conflict with their tyre supplier, Pirelli, who had lost interest in Formula One and had failed to keep up with the technical developments of their rivals, Goodyear and Michelin. At Imola the problems with Pirelli came to a head, and Senna failed to qualify for the race – the only time in his career that he suffered such a fate, and the moment at which he began to see his medium-term future elsewhere.

Perhaps, too, that hardened his attitude to a celebrity race at the new Nürburgring circuit in May, at which he joined a host of past and present stars, all driving identical Mercedes 190 saloons.

For most of them, it was a bit of a lark; for Senna, it was a chance to make another mark. In a twelve-lap sprint he beat Niki Lauda home by a second and a half, with the likes of Reutemann, Rosberg, Watson and Prost in his wake, along with such former heroes as Denny Hulme, Jody Scheckter, Jack Brabham, James Hunt, John Surtees, Phil Hill – six world champions – and Stirling Moss, the old champion emeritus. Some of them may not have approached the event in quite the same intense spirit as Senna, but the twenty-four-year-old took the opportunity to demonstrate his seriousness of purpose to an important captive audience.

He got the new Toleman, and some Michelin tyres fitted, and at the Monaco Grand Prix he arrived. As simple as that.

Thirteenth in practice on a dry track, he made the most of race-day rain. His own skill and other people's accidents saw him move up to second position by the twentieth of the scheduled seventy-eight laps. On a circuit noted for its lack of passing places, his victims were Jacques Laffite's Williams, Manfred Winkelhock's ATS, Keke Rosberg's Williams, Rene Arnoux's Ferrari and Niki Lauda's McLaren. While accidents were befalling such aces as Tambay, Warwick, Piquet and Mansell, Senna was not only keeping his car on the track but was circulating faster than anyone as the rain fell harder and harder. On lap twenty he was half a minute behind the leader, Alain Prost; over the next eleven laps he reduced the gap to seven and a half seconds.

But then, at the end of the thirty-second lap, with Senna closing fast on Prost and with forty-six laps still to go, it was suddenly all over. The clerk of the course, the former Ferrari driver Jacky Ickx, leaned out over the finish line holding a red flag. Senna caught Prost just before the line and completed the slowing-down lap believing he had won, only to be told on his arrival back at the pits that the rules said that the winner would be whoever had led at the end of the lap preceding the showing of the red flag. In other words, Prost was the winner by 7.4 seconds.

There was immediate controversy. Ickx claimed that the weather had been too bad for the race to continue in safety, but races had been run to a finish in such weather and worse (Ickx himself had come second at Monaco in a cloudburst in 1972); nor, by any means, did the roads of the Principality represent the worst place to race in the wet, given the comparatively low average speed and the high level of visual information offered to drivers by the natural features – buildings, advertising hoardings and so on – bordering the narrow roadway, which allowed an easier orientation in rain and spray than the empty expanses of an artificial autodrome. There were dark mutterings about Prost's nationality, and the fact that Monaco is practically in France, and the Belgian Ickx being a Francophone, and so on. Nevertheless, although deprived of his first grand prix victory by a very dubious decision, Senna behaved with perfect dignity. His restraint sent out the message that what he had done – and particularly the comparison with Prost, a more experienced driver at the wheel of a much better car – could be allowed to speak for itself. Which it did. 'I probably got more publicity than if I'd won,' he was later to say.

His showing raised Toleman's hopes, but the next few races were undistinguished enough to re-establish a mood of realism. Not until they reached Brands Hatch, for the British Grand Prix, was Senna again able to rise above the car's limitations. First, though, came a bad practice accident to Cecotto, who had been struggling vainly to match his team leader's speed all year. Senna had been fastest in the morning warm-up, and after only four minutes of the afternoon qualifying period Cecotto lost control in the fast Westfield Bend, hitting the barriers so hard that he had to be cut from the wreckage and taken to hospital by helicopter. The injuries to his ankles ended his Formula One career on the spot. Undaunted by Cecotto's misfortune, Senna qualified seventh. In the race he made steady progress through the field until, with two laps to go, he brought the crowd in the Paddock Bend grandstands to their feet by diving inside De Angelis to separate the Lotus team leader from third place. Senna was on the podium for the second time, and he had done it with a tactic refined at Brands Hatch in the Formula Ford years. The spectators loved it.

Now he had the Toleman running regularly just behind the élite, although it was seldom reliable. But before the Dutch Grand Prix in August, Michelin announced their withdrawal from grand prix racing, a bombshell for Toleman since the team had already fallen out with Goodyear, now the only remaining tyre supplier. Suddenly their new-found relative stability had been undermined again. At Zandvoort, it was destroyed.

A prematurely leaked press release on the headed paper of the Lotus team appeared in the paddock at the Dutch Grand Prix, announcing that Ayrton Senna would be joining them for 1985, replacing Mansell alongside De Angelis. There was consternation in the Toleman pit, followed by anger.

Alex Hawkridge was not surprised that Senna's thoughts had been roaming, given the degree of his ambition, but this was the first he had heard of any concrete plans, and the news of negotiations, never mind the apparent existence of a signed contract, clearly breached the terms of the buy-out clause in his deal with Senna, which stipulated that compensation had to be paid to Toleman before contact could be made with another team. Later it emerged that Senna's newly appointed manager, Armando Botelho, had been in clandestine contact with Lotus since early July, and that negotiations had been under way for two months. The intention had been to make the announcement at Zandvoort, but not until after Senna had broken the news to Toleman that he would be exercising the escape clause.

Denis Jenkinson of *Motor Sport*, the doyen of British grand prix correspondents and already a confirmed Senna fan, described the driver's behaviour as 'a simple case of bad manners and lack of discipline'. Harsh words were exchanged between the furious Hawkridge and his embarrassed driver. Senna claimed that he had been indicating since early in the season that he would be moving elsewhere. Hawkridge, in his rage, then did something that few team managers would have contemplated, given the powerful personality cults surrounding grand prix drivers. Infuriated by the patronizing tone of the Lotus press release, which included the statement that 'he (Senna) will, of course, continue to drive for Toleman for the rest of the season', Hawkridge announced that, as a punishment, the Brazilian would be suspended from the next round of the world championship, at Monza.

Before long Senna did indeed stump up the money stipulated in the buy-out clause, but the relationship could not be repaired in the course of the last two races of the season. At the Nürburgring, he qualified twelfth and went out of the race after colliding with Rosberg on the first lap, the cause of the accident disputed between Senna, who said Rosberg had turned into him on a corner, and the Finn, who believed Senna had simply left his braking too late. At Estoril, Senna redeemed himself by qualifying and finishing third, giving the team extra championship points – and according to the arcane system by which grand prix teams are remunerated, a reduction in travelling expenses for the next season.

Sadly, it would not be enough to secure the team's long-term prospects. Coming on the back of Cecotto's injury and the loss of Michelin, the messy conclusion to Senna's tenure discouraged the sponsors Hawkridge had been hoping to attract for the following season. They struggled on through a mediocre 1985, but then Ted Toleman himself decided that the game was up and sold the team lock, stock and barrel to the Italian clothing manufacturers Alessandro and Luciano Benetton, who used it as the foundation of the project that would one day also have a bearing on the destiny of Ayrton Senna.

By the time he got to Lotus, Senna was already several years too late. Had Colin Chapman not died in 1982, he and Senna might have reconstituted something like the partnership between the Lotus boss and Jim Clark in the sixties, when Chapman sent Clark out to conquer the world in tiny little green cigar-tubes that looked delicate enough to float away but were packed with ingenious engineering solutions. Chapman was a bold engineer, willing to take a risk – sometimes with other people's lives – in order to get an edge, and Senna would undoubtedly have responded to his single-minded ambition. Even after Clark's fatal accident at Hockenheim in 1968, Chapman's cars had carried Graham Hill, Jochen Rindt, Emerson Fittipaldi and Mario Andretti to the world title. But the founder's death took away his company's innovative genius, and nothing that Peter Warr or his own successors could do would prevent the onset of the gradual decline of the team which had once surpassed Ferrari in the total number of grand prix victories, into bankruptcy and closure at the beginning of 1995.

At the start of the 1985 season, however, such a fate seemed highly unlikely. The cars still carried the impressive black and gold livery of John Player Special cigarettes, the colours in which Fittipaldi and Andretti had won their titles. They were designed by a talented Frenchman, Gérard Ducarouge, and they were still enjoying the use of Renault engines which delivered plenty of horsepower, although their thirstiness was a problem in an era when the fuel regulations – born of a dim understanding of the outside world's growing 'green' consciousness – forced drivers to keep one eye on their opponents and the other on the petrol gauge.

Continuing what would become his traditional practice of starting off by putting pressure on his own team mate, so establishing his right to any preferential treatment that might be going, Senna led De Angelis, who was starting his sixth season with the team, until his ignition system failed. But in the second race of the season, at Estoril, Senna dominated the Portuguese Grand Prix in such a way as to adjust the whole ranking system of Formula One.

In qualifying he took his first Formula One pole position, more than a second faster than De Angelis. On the Sunday it poured, and the race was his. As the remainder of the field floundered around, he dominated the conditions to such an extent that even a trip off the circuit, with all four wheels on the grass as he accelerated down the hill behind the paddock, was handled with complete equanimity (he called it luck, but other people who saw the incident considered that this was the kind of luck you made for yourself). A full minute behind him came the Ferrari of Michele Alboreto, the only man Senna did not lap. As he returned to the pits, Senna greeted his crew with both hands off the wheel, double-punching the air in delight.

There was another pole at Imola, and a secure lead until the Renault ran dry with four laps to go; and at Monaco he led for the first thirteen laps until the consequences of over-revving the engine on the warm-up lap became evident. In the harsher streets of Detroit, he took pole and fought for the lead with Mansell's Williams until a tyre change put him back; he was up to third when he hit the wall. He was leading at Silverstone when the fuel injection packed up, and at the Nürburgring when the engine blew. A second place in Austria and thirds in Holland and Italy followed. Then the rain came again, allowing him to display his virtuosity at Spa-Francorchamps, the most awe-inspiring and demanding of all modern circuits, where the race went from wet to wetter to dry and he finished in front of Mansell and Prost. At a dry Brands Hatch he had to concede to Mansell, who won again in South Africa, where Senna's engine expired, as it did in the final race of the season, the inaugural Australian Grand Prix at Adelaide – after a strangely undisciplined performance during which he forced Mansell off the track at the first bend and then indulged in some provocative wheel-to-wheel stuff with Rosberg and others.

Prost took the title, his first, at the age of thirty. But Senna could look back on two wins, two seconds, two thirds, seven pole positions, ten front-row starts and thirty-eight points, enough to give him fourth place in the table, just ahead of his team mate, who had started the season as the number one. The yellow helmet was now a fixture at the front.

He had seen off De Angelis, who transferred his services to the Brabham team for 1986. Now Senna was the undisputed team leader, and he extended the terms of his status to the prerogative of choosing his own team mate – something few teams would have arrogated to a driver. Peter Warr and the rest of the team badly wanted to sign Derek Warwick, whose experience with Renault had been unhappy yet who would have come into the team with experience of the French engines that also powered the Lotuses. Warwick was fast, knowledgeable, enthusiastic and hard working. His nationality was also an asset as far as the team were concerned: a British team with a British sponsor needed a British driver, as long as he was quick enough to give good support to the number one.

In Senna's eyes, Warwick was too quick, too experienced, and too likely to divert the team's attention from what was, to him, its only real task: preparing a car in which he could win the world championship. To Senna, Lotus did not have the resources to match what McLaren were doing for Prost and Lauda. He put his foot down and, at the age of twenty-five and with only two grand prix victories behind him, he prevailed over the wishes of a team that had been a fixture since 1958 and had seventy-five wins to its name. Back-pedalling at high speed, Warr instead signed Johnny Dumfries, who had graduated through Formula Ford and Formula Three but was in no position to get in Senna's way either on or off the track. As for Senna, this was his first experience of the righteous wrath of the British motor racing press, which was collectively fond of Warwick (so much more congenial in their eyes than Mansell, whom they perceived as a humourless whinger). They wanted to see Warwick in a good car, and went for the Brazilian in a big way when he seemed to be exercising a seigneurial right at the expense of their man.

Senna had always seemed slightly aloof, certainly towards those he considered his rivals. Now, as he explained why he thought that Lotus couldn't cope with two star drivers, his measured articulacy in a foreign language served not to convince the reporters (and, by extension, their readers), so much as to harden a growing view of him as a ruthless, high-handed man whose ambition was running amok.

Frustratingly, 1986 went much the way of 1985: eight pole positions and two more wins, at Jerez and Detroit, but the chances of more were again spoilt by the Renault engine's insistence on gulping down its fuel. Yet at Jerez, Senna provided one of the most exciting finishes in grand prix history. Mansell, with whom he had been jousting throughout the race, found himself having to make almost twenty seconds back on Senna in the last eight laps after a pit stop, failing to catch the Brazilian by only 0.014 sec.; only once had a smaller winning margin been recorded. There was another memorable duel in the inaugural Hungarian Grand Prix in Budapest, this time against Piquet, who made angry protests against what he considered to be Senna's over-aggressive tactics.

But the car was running out of petrol all over the place, which disillusioned Renault, who hated seeing vehicles with their name on the side limping to a halt in front of many millions of television spectators. That was why they had disbanded their own team at the end of the previous season; now, at the end of 1986, they withdrew their engines from Formula One altogether.

Prost won his second successive championship in the thrifty McLaren-TAG Porsche, but his new partner, Keke Rosberg, had proved a spent force. Mansell and Piquet were second and third, their combined efforts amassing enough points to give Williams the constructors' title even though by fighting each other to the death for the drivers' championship they had effectively killed off each other's chances. Senna was again fourth: for him, not good enough.

With one year left on his Lotus contract, he was encouraged by the news that Warr had secured the same Honda engines as Williams for 1987. This was something of a negative victory, since the Japanese company's relationship with Williams had deteriorated.

Honda were displeased with Frank Williams's apparent inability to impose team orders on Mansell and Piquet. Unquestionably, such liberal treatment had cost them the drivers' title: a reward carrying far more prestige than the constructors' cup. And Honda's view of the team was also coloured by the mid-season car accident which had befallen Frank Williams. Hurrying back to Nice airport from a testing session at Le Castellet, he had rolled his hire car and damaged his spine to such an extent that he would never again have the use of his arms and legs. Maybe they thought that this would finish him; they should have asked Ron Dennis, who believed that the consequences of the accident, and the restrictions on Williams's range of activities, would only serve to concentrate his mind more closely on the job of winning races.

At any rate, now Williams would lose their exclusive use of Honda's enormously powerful engines. And arriving at Lotus as part of the deal came, at the manufacturer's behest, a new team-mate for Senna. Satoru Nakajima was the first Japanese driver to take a regular part in Formula One. Another in the Dumfries mould, he would provide loyal, competent, reliable and unspectacular support, as well as useful experience gained from his stint as a Honda test driver. Out of the scene along with Renault went the team's main sponsors, Imperial Tobacco, ending a relationship stretching back to 1968. In came another brand of cigarettes, Camel.

The new all-yellow livery provided a poor sort of setting for the yellow helmet, an apt reflection of a season in which the team made their last real attempt to live up to Chapman's standards of innovation in engineering. The new Lotus-Honda 99T incorporated the first computer-controlled 'active' suspension system, created to dictate the behaviour of the chassis in relation to the track in a way that made the car's passage more efficient and therefore, or so it was intended, faster. Here was the birth of the generation of computerized driver-aids that within six years would lead to fears that the human pilot could be dispensed with altogether (and to rumours that at least one leading Formula One team boss was actively pursuing the possibility, anxious to reduce his wage bill and eliminate the time spent negotiating with prima

77

donnas). Chapman would have loved all that. But he would have hated the fact that, unlike his own lightweight designs, the 99T was as sleek as a double-decker bus.

In fact it needed the human skills of an Ayrton Senna to make it function at anything like a competitive level. All the benefits of the Japanese horsepower were undermined by its bulk and poor aerodynamics. Nevertheless he managed to lead the opening race at Rio briefly, before something broke. At Imola he took pole but could not hold off the Williams of Mansell, to whom he finished second.

The two of them battled again at Imola, until they touched wheels and spun off. Mansell got back on to the circuit, but when he retired a few laps later he leapt from his car and muscled his way into Senna's pit, where he had to be pulled away by the Lotus mechanics, some of whom had worked with the Englishman during his time with the team. 'When a man holds you round the throat, I do not think he has come to apologize,' Senna said drily afterwards. Their versions of the incident differed wildly, as so many would throughout the remainder of Senna's career. 'I was pushed off the circuit,' Mansell said. 'I couldn't believe what he was trying to do – overtake at a place like that,' Senna countered.

They were together again on the front row at Monaco, but a turbo failure on Mansell's car handed Senna the first of his two wins that season. The second came in Detroit, where Mansell, after leading, was slowed by various problems. Now Senna was leading the championship, but it was already clear that the Williams was making better use of the Honda power than the Lotus. Over the rest of the season Senna could claim only three second places and two thirds as other teams made progress and the Lotus gradually became less competitive. By the time they got to Mexico City in October, he was so frustrated that when he spun off during a battle with Piquet, he clouted an official who had tried to prevent him getting an illegal push start and was fined $15,000.

As is the way in Formula One, where most business is done

behind the back of the hand, Senna had been talking to Ron Dennis about a move to McLaren since before the season's halfway point. And when Peter Warr opened a letter from the Brazilian's representatives early in August, announcing his intention to go elsewhere for the next year, the Lotus boss decided to move quickly to stage a pre-emptive strike and thereby prevent Senna's negotiations with other teams dictating the movement of the entire driver market.

Piquet, heading for his third world championship in a Williams set-up where he now held sway, was not intending to stay with the team. He knew that they were finally losing their Honda engines altogether, and that Honda wanted him to maintain their relationship by moving to Lotus. So, encouraged by the Japanese, Warr signed him up and announced his swift coup straight away, without telling Senna privately first. It was a very public slap in the face for Senna, who was quick to broadcast his distaste for what he considered a breach of etiquette. He had a point, although he had been guilty of something similar at Toleman and could hardly complain. But what really irked him was that he had been outmanoeuvred. Instead of appearing to dictate his own destiny, he had been made to look foolish – as if he were being replaced by a more valuable property, the reigning world champion.

As with the Toleman punishment, however, there was never much doubt over who would really feel the pain. Senna was moving to McLaren, where Prost's authority appeared to be undisputed after his back-to-back championships (the first since Brabham a quarter of a century earlier), but which would also be receiving the prized Honda engines for 1988. And Senna, too, now had a good relationship with Honda, which would help neutralize the advantage of Prost's familiarity with the McLaren team. The Japanese, with a Brazilian ace at each team, were on to a winner either way.

And at McLaren, Senna also got the chance to develop a rapport with Ron Dennis, who felt that his failure to offer the young driver a tempting deal back in 1983 represented the biggest mistake of his career. Dennis and Senna were made for each other: both eloquent, clear-eyed, persuasive, proud, fastidious, utterly committed to whatever success required, either in commercial or engineering terms.

Dennis is, however, a hard man to love; or at least his team can sometimes be. The aura of corporate success, the obsession with order and neatness, can be off-putting. Nothing could be further from the old Battle of Britain pit culture of oily rags and greasy chips. Spend an hour in the McLaren pit while the mechanics are working flat-out, and you will not see a single drop of oil. Presumably the sponsors wouldn't like it; or maybe the cars don't need oil any more.

Dennis tells a story about their negotiations over the 1988 contract that says something about the world in which he and Senna were moving. Eventually, he explains, the difference between them boiled down to a matter of half a million dollars. They couldn't agree. They went on disagreeing. And finally, to break the deadlock, Dennis suggested that they toss a coin for it. Senna, he says, didn't understand the concept of tossing coins. Dennis explained it to him, with some difficulty. Eventually it got through. Senna called, and called wrong. So Dennis was better off by half a million dollars.

But what Senna hadn't realized, Dennis says with cool relish, is that it was half a million dollars *a season*. So the gamble had, in fact, cost Senna a million and a half. Dennis gives his cool, thin-lipped smile. What a joke. A rich man's joke. The kind of thing you might overhear in the lounge at Sandy Lane or the bar at San Lorenzo, late at night. Doesn't necessarily transfer well to the world outside.

John Watson, too, has a story about a conversation with Senna just before the start of the 1988 season. You raced for McLaren with Prost, Senna said. Tell me about him. Well, Watson replied, you'd do well to bear in mind that the whole team think of Prost as the number one, and they work the way he wants them to work. If you take my advice, you'll have a close look at his methods, because that's how the team function. Senna paused a moment, thinking about it. No, he said finally, that's not how I'm going to do it. I'm going to make him come to me. 'I'm going to blitz him,' Senna concluded.

He blitzed him all right. Six pole positions in a row, starting with the first race of the season, gave Alain Prost the message. Ayrton Senna was now unquestionably the world's fastest driver, a claim that can rarely be made with much confidence, given the difficulty of making direct comparisons between men in different teams.

Neither man's car had turned a wheel before leaving the pit lane for the first practice session at the newly rechristened Autódromo Nelson Piquet in Rio; even the spare car had done only 300 miles. The McLaren-Honda MP4/4 was an untested commodity. Yet by Saturday night Senna was on pole, ahead of Mansell, with Prost third.

On the warm-up lap, Senna's gear linkage played up. He drove into the pits, jumped into the spare car, and started the race from the pit lane, at the back of the field. After fighting his way up to second place, a flat battery dropped him to sixth. He was girding himself for another assault when he was told that a change of car after the parade lap was against the rules. He was disqualified, leaving Prost to motor serenely on to victory, as he had so often done. The greatest battle of their lives had begun.

Chapter Seven

It was just before the Rio meeting that an interview with Nelson Piquet appeared in a local paper, in which he suggested that Senna was the sort of fellow who wasn't keen on girls. Piquet mentioned that he knew it for a fact, because his current girlfriend had gone out with Senna and would testify to his preferences.

The general impression was that Piquet had gone beyond the limits of acceptable insult. Then, however, he went practically out of sight. During the course of a second interview, in the Brazilian edition of *Playboy* published just as the teams were gathering in Rio, Piquet made a further series of gratuitously unpleasant comments about some of his fellow racers. Mansell, he said, was 'an uneducated fool with a stupid and ugly wife'. Piquet's naughty-boy charm suddenly looked like brattishness. Something rather nasty was happening to Formula One.

Senna was all for taking legal action on the basis of the first interview, until a quiet word from a sponsor persuaded him that it would do more harm than good.

Several women came forward to dispel the shadow cast by Piquet's insults. 'If that man is gay, then I'd like to have a gay in my bed every night,' said twenty-four-year-old Surama Castro, a model who spent some time with Senna after meeting him at Milan's Malpensa airport. 'Piquet just wants all the girls Senna has that he can't get,' added Maria Cristina Mendes Caldeira, a long-time platonic friend in São Paulo.

Later in the year Senna embarked on a two-year affair with Xuxa Meneghel, a hugely popular singer and presenter of children's television shows in Brazil. This appears to have been the most serious of his relationships during the time between Liliane

Vasconcelos Souza, his wife, and Adriane Galisteu, the girlfriend of his last year.

His family liked Xuxa, but the nation's immoderate enthusiasm may not have helped. She was the woman Brazil wanted him to marry: they were Mick Jagger and Marianne Faithfull, or Paul McCartney and Jane Asher. And similarly destined to disappoint a sentimental public.

His other girlfriends occupied much shorter spans of his time than the three big relationships. Among those with whom his name was linked were Virgínia Nowicki, Marjorie Andrade, Patrícia Machado, Cristine Ferraciu, Marcella Prado and the actress Carol Alt. Meneghel and Alt apart, he did not appear to care for the companionship of fellow celebrities; although he was sometimes glimpsed with them in gossip magazines, in general he stayed out of the paparazzi's way. And only once was there a real scandal: when Marcella Prado, a Rio model, claimed that during the course of their single date she had conceived his daughter, whom she called Vitoria.

What the fuss did achieve was to add a further layer of mystery to the deepening impression of Senna as an unusually complex character among the community of sports stars, most of whom are not noted for their ability to distinguish, as he certainly was, between introspection and self-obsession.

In pure sports terms, his motivation – his 'focusing', to use the jargon – was unsurpassed not just in its intensity but in its consistency. Senna never cruised, never backed off, never settled for what fate had given him that afternoon. But there was a remoteness about him that compelled a different degree of attention. The level of personal control was fascinating. 'Friday, Saturday, the eve of a grand prix,' his last girlfriend was to say, 'Ayrton would put on his helmet and overalls and turn into Senna.' The control was even more riveting, and sometimes chilling, when it started to fray. However reprehensible the cause or the response, it revealed the existence of his humanity.

His religion was at the centre of all this. On long-haul flights to and from the races, he would sit in the first-class compartment with his head buried in the Bible.

'I am able to experience God's presence on earth,' he once said. But his faith was not part of a collective manifestation. 'If I go to church, I go on my own and I like to be there alone. I find more peace that way.'

His Christianity had nothing to do with smiling, back-slapping, born-again evangelism. It needed work, like everything else. Inevitably, it was misunderstood and mocked: 'It hurts me if things come out such as I have a feeling that I am unbeatable or even immortal because of my belief in God. What I said was that God gives me strength, but also that life is a present that God has given to us and that we are obliged to keep it, to handle it carefully.'

His faith was about individual self-realization, and it did not exclude feelings of anger, resentment and revenge. What it did was provide him with an armour of self-belief so effective that while it could not prevent him feeling the pain of insults, it ensured that no wound was deep enough to shake his composure or force him to doubt the decisions he had taken.

Perhaps this made him appear more aloof than he really was. Brazil represented his sanctuary; only there could he relax completely. He had moved his European base from a house in Esher, acquired during his time with Toleman, to an apartment in Monaco, a predictable choice for an established grand prix driver, given the tax breaks and the geographical convenience. But his absolute priority was to fly back to São Paulo at every opportunity. At home with his family on the farm at Goiás, with his nephew and nieces, with his girlfriends, serenity came easily in tennis, water-skiing, go-karting, listening to Phil Collins, Genesis, Freddie Mercury and Tina Turner, collecting belts (bought by the dozen from airport duty-free shops), flying his model aeroplanes and helicopters. Later he would have his own apartment in São Paulo, and beach houses in Portugal and Brazil.

Apart from the amount of money they cost, these are simple, ordinary, undemanding things: banal enough to embody the aspirations of his fans. Only in its spiritual and philosophical dimensions did the surface of his life betray the existence of a complex, unique and demanding talent.

At Imola, he quickly readjusted the position within his own team, leading Prost home in the first of ten McLaren one-twos that season, a degree of domination that recalled the days of Fangio, Moss and the omnipotent Mercedes team of the mid-fifties. Both cars lapped the rest of the field. And then they came to Monaco, his new adopted home, where he set out to dominate a meeting which was to provide a turning point in the development of his personal philosophy.

His experience that weekend only became known two years later, when he described it to the Canadian journalist Gerald Donaldson. People have tried to get metaphysical about motor racing in the past, but here Senna took it into a new realm. Which was where it had taken him.

'Sometimes I think I know some of the reasons why I do the things the way I do in a car and sometimes I think I don't know why,' he was telling Donaldson. 'There are some moments that seem to be the natural instinct that is in me. Whether I have been born with it or whether this feeling has grown in me more than other people I don't know, but it is inside me and it takes over with a great amount of space and intensity. When I am competing against the watch and against other competitors, the feeling of expectation, of getting it done and doing the best I can gives me a kind of power that some moments when I am driving actually detaches me completely from anything else as I am doing it . . . corner after corner, lap after lap. I can give you a true example.

'Monte Carlo '88, the last qualifying session. I was already on pole and I was going faster and faster. One lap after the other, quicker and quicker and quicker. I was at one stage just on pole, then by half a second and then one second and I just kept going. Suddenly I was nearly two seconds faster than anybody else, including my team mate with the same car. And suddenly I realized that I was no longer driving the car consciously. I was driving it by a kind of instinct, only I was in a different dimension. It was like I was in a tunnel. Not only the tunnel under the hotel but the whole circuit was a tunnel. I was just going and going, more and more and more and more. I was way over the limit but still able to find even more.

'Then suddenly something just kicked me. I kind of woke up and realized that I was in a different atmosphere than you normally are. My immediate reaction was to back off, slow down. I drove back slowly to the pits and I didn't want to go out any more that day. It frightened me because I was well beyond my conscious understanding. It happens rarely but I keep these experiences very much alive inside me because it is something that is important for self-preservation.'

You can listen to that, and dismiss it. Or you can say, yes, perhaps this is the sort of thing that happens to people who operate at a very high level of mental and physical activity, where the intellect and the body combine and it becomes hard to say which is pulling the strings. To me Senna's words recall the sensation experienced by an improvising musician who reaches the point at which technique falls away and the execution becomes virtually automatic, leaving no barrier between the artist and the expression. The distinguished American saxophonist Steve Lacy took on the burden of putting it into words in conversation with another improviser, the English guitarist Derek Bailey, and his description has many parallels with Senna's. 'I'm attracted to improvisation because of something I value,' Lacy said. 'That is a freshness, a certain quality, which can only be obtained by improvisation, something you cannot possibly get from writing. It is something to do with the "edge". Always being on the brink of the unknown and being prepared for the leap. And when you go on out there you have all your years of preparation and all your sensibilities and your prepared means, but it is a leap into the unknown. If through that leap you find something, then it has a value which I don't think can be found any other way. I place a higher value on that than on what you can prepare. But I am also hooked into what you can prepare, especially in the way that it can take you to the edge. What I write is to take you to the edge safely so that you can go out there and find this other stuff . . .'

Stuck with their printed scores, the other competitors recognized something beyond the normal realms of great skill in Senna's speed, although they would probably have avoided discussion of the mystical dimension. 'The attitude of most people,' the pragmatic Denis Jenkinson wrote in *Motor Sport*, describing the mood on the eve of the race, 'was to try not to be lapped by Senna too often.' And when the race started on a warm and dry afternoon, Senna and the McLaren simply drove off into the distance, leaving the remaining cars – including Prost, who had also started from the front row – to race among themselves. With twenty-five laps to go the red and white cars were first and second again, separated by a large gap, and Ron Dennis sent an order over the radio for them to ease off. But slowing down, as somebody once said, was not in Senna's vocabulary, and the mere introduction of the idea may have contributed to what happened next.

On lap sixty-seven, with eleven left to the certainty of his second Monaco win, Senna flicked the McLaren nimbly through the left and right of Casino Square, hustled it down the short, bumpy chute to Mirabeau and tweaked it around the Loews Hotel hairpin. Then, just as he had done with perfect ease sixty-six times that afternoon, he dropped the car down towards the seafront, and the sharp right-handed corner called Portier, where the coast road enters the long, dark tunnel, the fastest part of the circuit. And for once, his mind wandered. He groped for the edge, and lost it.

What he did was turn in too tightly, allowing his right nose-fin to clip the barrier on the apex of the corner; this threw him across the track, where his left front wheel hit the opposite barrier with enough force to bend back the suspension and stop the car. The TV camera that caught the next few moments showed him leaping angrily from the machine, pushing away the track marshals, pulling off his helmet, tossing his earplugs to the ground and stalking out of the circuit as Prost motored by to take, yet again, the race around the houses that should have been Senna's.

He didn't go back to the pits, or to the McLaren garage in the paddock. He disappeared. All evening, in his apartment, the phone was answered by his housekeeper, who refused to put callers through. When, long after nightfall, she relented, the friend who spoke to him discovered that he was still in tears.

To most drivers, an accident that does not involve personal injury is just an accident, even when it costs them a grand prix. It is something to be forgotten. Not by Senna, though. When he had an accident, it became an event with a real meaning, with a subtext beneath its narrative significance. Of Monaco 1989 he was to say: 'It has changed my life.'

No driver played mind games with more commitment and ferocity than Senna, who drew on his older sister, Viviane, a psychologist, for counsel. 'I am the same person,' he said after Monaco, 'but my mental strength has changed.' He knew that in a sport such as motor racing, where willingness to risk life and limb in straight combat is the essence of the whole thing, an ability to put his opponents at a psychological disadvantage would be worth as much as a few extra horsepower. 'You have to be strong psychologically speaking, very tough, to go through the kind of war that goes on sometimes,' he observed on another occasion, speaking with the limpid intensity that characterized his pronouncements.

That's what he meant in later years when, analysing his own rise, he claimed that 'nothing had come easy' to him. In his view, such a statement was not in conflict with his privileged background, or with his father's material and spiritual support, since it referred to the mental struggle he had undergone in order to become as good as he was, and then to maintain the exercise of his supremacy. This meant an unremitting engagement in mental battles: to lose any fight, whether to a rival on the track or to his own team manager during a contract negotiation, put him at risk of dulling the edge of his gift.

As the years went by, Senna spoke more and more freely about the mental side of racing. His ability to bring his intellect to bear on the preparation of a racing car was already legendary: the mechanics at Toleman and Lotus had been sorry to see him go, because he cared as much as they did, he worked as hard, and he thanked them at the end of a long day. They knew, too, that if they found something, some little adjustment, that would give him another half-second a lap, his talent would turn it into a full second. When he focused on their problems, nothing – no intrusion from the glamorous side of a racing driver's life – would be allowed to distract him. That told them that he knew how important they were. And to them he was the answer to a prayer. He could tell his race engineers about the behaviour of each of the car's four wheels at every corner on all the laps of a practice session; once the engineers had come to understand the degree of his total recall and the accuracy of his impressions, they could compare his subjective views with the cold data accumulated from the car's telemetry, its onboard computers, and then plot their technical solutions in response to both types of input. Best of all, unlike some of his contemporaries, he never blamed his own failures on imaginary mechanical faults, or exaggerated the problems that did exist in order to put his own performance in a better light.

Senna and McLaren were still finding out about each other, but the Brazilian won in Detroit and then reeled off four victories in a row: at Silverstone, Hockenheim, the Hungaroring and Spa-Francorchamps. The British race became the first of the season at which a McLaren had not led on the opening lap when Berger's Ferrari came round first in heavy rain and stayed there until Senna overtook him after fourteen laps. Prost, not enjoying the conditions, pulled off before half-distance and gave up, leaving the crowd to enjoy an extended demonstration of Senna's touch and commitment on the wet track. In Germany there was rain again on race day, but Prost, stung by criticism in the French newspapers of his Silverstone performance, stuck to his task and finished fourteen seconds behind.

By the time they got to Monza, the rivalry was building to a crescendo. Senna took his ninth pole of the season, beating one of Jim Clark's long-standing records, and set off with victory in mind. Prost retired early and it was left to the home team, the Ferraris of Gerhard Berger and Michele Alboreto, to attempt to put pressure on the surviving McLaren. This was the first grand prix to be held since the death of the Old Man, Enzo Ferrari, who, rightly or wrongly, had come to be revered around the world as the embodiment of motor racing's romantic tradition. All around the circuit, 80,000 Italian fans waved their flags to urge the red cars on. But with two laps to go it seemed that Senna was in no danger as, well in the lead, he came up to lap the Williams of Jean-Louis Schlesser at the first chicane after the pits.

Schlesser, an experienced driver but now making his first appearance in Formula One as a temporary replacement for the absent Mansell, would have been less aware than anyone in the field of the meaning of the yellow helmet in his mirrors. He might have been aware that it was Senna, but he could have no experience of the rate at which Senna would be catching him up. As the McLaren loomed behind him, Schlesser was anyway otherwise engaged in the business of trying to overtake Mauricio Gugelmin's March. Unusually, Senna failed to appreciate the implications. He dived for the inside, intending to outbrake the Williams, Schlesser turned in, the McLaren slid off into the sand, and with it went Ron Dennis's hopes of winning all sixteen races that season. The astonished Ferrari drivers screamed over the line and took the race, with the fans in delirium.

In Hungary Senna and Prost fought hand to hand, the Brazilian just hanging on. In Belgium Senna led from start to finish. Now the championship was poised: Senna with seventy-five points, Prost seventy-two, the rest nowhere.

It was at Estoril that the relationship – characterized by Senna only a couple of months earlier as an example of 'harmony, not friction' – began to turn nasty. Here Prost outqualified Senna, but the Brazilian took the lead off the line. Coming round at the end of the first lap, however, Prost slipped out from Senna's slipstream in a classic high-speed overtaking manoeuvre, only to find Senna squeezing him right over to the pit wall. The crews, leaning over to watch the cars go by, flinched as Prost brushed the concrete. The moment was bloodcurdling, unbelievable in real life.

'It was dangerous,' a horrified Prost said afterwards, hardly molli-fied by the fact that he had won the race after various problems pushed Senna down to sixth. 'If he wants the world championship that badly, he can have it.'

Senna virtually ignored his complaints, suggesting only that he had been angered by Prost forcing him on to the grass at the start. But of all the examples of Senna's aggressive behaviour in his Formula One career to date, this was the one which most clearly carried into the grown-up world the Formula Ford playground tactics of weaving, crowding, barging and general intimidation. Had the cars touched at that moment in Estoril, the great crash at Le Mans in 1955 might have looked like a minor affair. Still, they didn't. Senna had not yet turned grand prix racing into a contact sport. That would come later.

So ended the co-operation between the two drivers. In Senna's mind, the harmony had never been real. He needed to dominate the thoughts of the team, to have them working solely for him. Now they knew not only which of the two was the faster driver, but also which was the more determined to go to the limit.

By the time they came to the last two races, at Suzuka and Adelaide, the way the championship worked out was that Senna needed only to win the first of them to take the title. If Prost won, the contest would continue to Adelaide. Given the ill feeling now simmering between the two, the president of Honda felt it necessary to issue a statement, in the form of an open letter to Jean-Marie Balestre, president of the FIA, reassuring the world's Formula One fans that his company would see fair play by giving Prost and Senna equal equipment, and an even chance to win.

When the red light turned to green at Suzuka, sitting on the pole with a greasy track ahead of him, the hyped-up Senna committed a novice's mistake: he stalled the engine. The field streamed past him as he raised his arms in the air to alert those coming from the back. But the start line at Suzuka is on a slight downslope, and as the car rolled forwards he got it restarted in time to enter the first corner in fourteenth place. By the end of the lap, he was eighth. On lap twenty-seven he was overtaking Prost, the leader, as they came on to the finishing straight. But the Frenchman stayed with him, and as the rain began again Senna was suddenly pointing to the sky as he passed the pits, a clear attempt to tell the officials that the race should be stopped. Prost, who had just beaten him at Monaco in 1984 as the result of a famously disputed stoppage, did not have time to smile at the irony. They were racing as fast as the track and their fuel consumption would let them, one man knowing that victory would give him the title, the other knowing that if he won, it would keep him in with a chance.

Senna stayed ahead. And as he accelerated out of the chicane towards the chequered flag and his first world championship, many thousands of miles from home and twenty-four years from the day his father gave him his first little go-kart, he raised his eyes from the grey tarmac and saw something. According to his own later account, he saw God.

The season over, Senna went home to celebrate his championship. There were formal receptions to attend, and days playing the go-karts on the family farm. But already he and Prost, with whom he was scheduled to resume a troubled relationship, had been testing the new McLaren-Honda MP4/5, which was to give Senna his first experience of a non-turbo Formula One car since the brief tests with Williams and McLaren six years earlier.

A lucky win for Mansell on his Ferrari début opened the 1989 season at Rio. Senna collided with Berger's Ferrari at the first corner as the two of them and Patrese's Williams all tried to occupy the same piece of track. 'Senna chopped across twice to try to make me back off,' Berger said, 'but he shouldn't try that with me. Never in my life will I back off in that situation.'

There was more controversy at Imola. First Berger disastrously lost control at Tamburello, probably as a result of losing part of his front wing. He crossed the narrow strip of grass and the few yards of tarmac, and hit the wall at 170 m.p.h. The car was immediately engulfed by flames. Berger sat in the inferno for twenty-three and a half seconds before astonishingly effective work by the Italian marshals put the fire out, enabling the Austrian to discharge himself the next day from the Ospedale Maggiore in Bologna with nothing more grave than a broken shoulder blade, a cracked rib and sternum, and harsh burns to his hands and chest.

The result of the race, which had to be restarted, was another McLaren demonstration: Senna first, Prost second. But the predictability of the result hid a conflict which flared into the open afterwards. The two of them, it was revealed, had made a perfectly sensible pact that whoever led into the first corner should not be challenged by the other during the opening laps. Ron Dennis, like Enzo Ferrari and Frank Williams, was not in the habit of issuing team orders, partly because a bit of creative tension never did a superstar any harm; nor is curbing natural aggression the best way to realize a promising youngster's potential. This informal 'accord', Prost said afterwards, had been Senna's idea. At the first start, the Brazilian had led and held his advantage, but when Prost got away quickest on the restart, Senna had whipped past him halfway round the first lap. The Frenchman's furious pursuit of him for the rest of the race was the product of pique, of the feeling that the Brazilian had cheated him. Prost left the circuit in a rage, skipping the mandatory press conference, and that was the end not merely of co-operation but of communication between the McLaren drivers. By comparison with what was to come, however, it was a squabble in a playpen.

First, Ron Dennis announced that all was well again, because Senna had apologized to Prost. Then Senna himself gave a long explanation in which he suggested that he had apologized only at Dennis's behest, and now considered he had been wrong to do so. He alleged that a similar agreement had been in force the previous year, but that Prost had broken it on several occasions as the season went on. But they had patched it up over the winter, and when he had asked what Prost wanted to do about the first bend at Imola in 1989, the Frenchman had replied: 'The same as '88.' Then Senna explained how he had indeed lagged behind at the start, but had gained speed faster and could hardly have been expected to slow down at that point in order to let Prost go, and in any case the agreement only covered overtaking under braking: 'We're in races, yes or no?' Yes, in which case no 'accord' is worth the breath with which it is spoken. But Dennis had said to him that if he apologized, it would be all over. 'And I did it. It was stupid because it meant I had changed my opinion on the concept of our accord and on the overtaking move. Now, I have never changed my opinion. I said sorry for the good of the team, to calm it down, because I was almost compelled to. I wiped away a tear because at that moment it was harming me.'

Prost's retort was instant: 'At the level of technical discussion I shall not close the door completely, but for the rest I no longer wish to have any business with him. I appreciate honesty and he is not honest.'

In Monaco, Senna managed quite well without his team-mate's conversation, leading all the way, with Prost almost a minute behind. In Mexico, Senna turned away from his team-mate's attempt at a rapprochement and won again, with Prost fifth. At

Phoenix he beat Jim Clark's twenty-one-year-old career record of thirty-three pole positions but retired from the lead, handing Prost the race. At Montreal, in a storm, he drove through the field and was heading for one of his greatest victories when he felt his engine faltering with three laps to go. Prost won at Paul Ricard, and again at Silverstone – where the British fans cheered when Senna spun out of the lead early on. They had admired Senna's sheer talent in his early years, but now they were starting to react against what they perceived to be a cold, manipulative personality, a profile which gained definition in contrast with Prost's relatively sunny, co-operative temperament.

To satisfy the requirements of the newspapers, who saw the circulation value of an old-fashioned shoot-out, particularly one that could be prolonged over a period of several months, the rivalry needed to be susceptible to simple moral judgements: Black Hat v White Hat. The casting was obvious. Senna, who rarely smiled in public and approached his task with a Jesuitical concentration, versus Prost, the family man with the crooked nose and funny corkscrew hair who had a bit of the Henri Leconte about him and looked as if he might not be averse to a Gauloise and a glass of Burgundy after the show. That they functioned in a world of uncertainties, of fragile etiquette, opaque rules and unfathomable technology, made the storyline all the more compelling.

Senna won at Hockenheim and dominated a wet Spa. At that point, the disillusioned Prost announced that he would be leaving McLaren at the end of the season to join Ferrari. At Monza he was welcomed with open arms by the Italian crowd, but Senna, the new villain, outqualified him by almost two seconds, a humiliation that led the Frenchman to charge his team with favouritism. 'You have to understand they don't make engines like this for Ayrton,' he said, raising again the spectre of Honda's technicians inserting different microchips in each motor, or perhaps – and people were beginning to believe this sort of thing, because it could be done – adjusting them during the race, maybe even via satellite transmission from the engine laboratory in Japan. Dennis issued a denial which gathered credibility when Senna's engine blew near the end and Prost took the victory. Nevertheless the Frenchman could not resist expressing his distaste for the team he was leaving by leaning down from the podium and handing the trophy to the adoring fans. Dennis, proud of his trophy cabinet, was livid.

Portugal was the race at which Mansell overshot his pit, reversed, and failed to see the black flags indicating his disqualification. Unfortunately he was still in ignorance of the futility of his effort when he came up to overtake Senna, with predictable results. Dennis was just in the act of telling Senna over the radio that Mansell had been disqualified and was no longer a factor in the race when the two of them collided and spun off, Mansell having tried to force himself through on the inside line. The usual post-race disagreements were coloured by the belief that not only should Mansell not have been on the inside line, he should not have been on the track at all.

An unchallenged win for Senna in the next race, at Jerez, set up the last two races for the championship. Prost was twenty-four points ahead on aggregate, but could still be caught under the scoring system if Senna won both the remaining events.

Prost drove with the brilliance of his best years at Suzuka, holding the lead against Senna's sustained attack until lap forty-seven, when the Brazilian tried a run down the inside into the ridiculously tight chicane. As they braked together, Prost began to pull across, turning in late, not quite on the line he would have used in practice, say, with no other traffic around. But Senna was alongside, practically level, and the two of them slid idiotically, uselessly, interlocked at a pathetically low speed, off the racing surface and on to the escape road behind the chicane's barriers.

Time stopped for a moment as they looked across at each other. Prost thought: if we're both out, the title is mine. He flipped open the catch of his safety straps, jumped out and walked away. Senna thought: if I'm out, it's over. Let's keep going. Waving the marshals to push him round, he turned the car back on to the track and headed for the pits, where a new nosecone was fitted and he resumed the desperate pursuit of victory.

Given the way their respective characters were being represented, the general belief in the aftermath was that Senna had taken a typically arrogant risk, and that Prost had behaved with complete correctness, if not prudence. But in the light of their words and actions in later years, when time and events had loosened their tongues, it seemed that Prost had indeed decided that having an accident – a nice civilized low-speed one – was the way to end the duel, if that was how Senna wanted to play it.

The chicane, Senna said afterwards, was 'the only place where I could overtake, and somebody who shouldn't have been there just closed the door and that was that.'

Whatever the rights and wrongs, Senna's choice of language was highly revealing. 'Somebody who shouldn't have been there': if he shouldn't have been there, then he didn't exist, so he didn't even have the right to a name, an identity. And if he didn't exist, then he couldn't have been there in the first place, so . . .

'You know Ayrton's problem?' Prost asked. 'He can't accept not winning, and because of that he can't accept someone resisting his overtaking manoeuvres. Too many times he tries to intimidate someone out of his way.' Now the tactics of Formula Ford had not only come to Formula One, but had taken over.

Senna regained the lead in the race, but was disqualified afterwards for missing out the chicane when he restarted. He lodged an appeal, on the basis that others had missed chicanes during the season with impunity. 'The results as they stand provisionally do not reflect the truth of the race in either the sporting sense or the sense of the regulations,' he said.

His action kept the championship notionally alive until Adelaide. But before the race FISA, the governing body, announced that he had been given a six-month suspended sentence and a $100,000 fine. He was distraught. 'When everything goes against you, you ask yourself why you carry on, particularly when you have not been fairly treated.' But, he added, he would continue to drive the way he had driven all his career. 'I am supposed to be a lunatic, a dangerous man breaking all the rules, but people have the wrong impression. What happened at Suzuka reflects the political situation in the sport. I'm prepared to fight to the end for my values, for justice.'

At Adelaide, in clouds of rain and spray, Prost had no qualms about pulling out on the second lap, winning the championship with a perfectly sound car in his garage. Senna took the lead, but hit the rear of Martin Brundle's slow Brabham as he came up to lap it, lost a wheel and was forced to retire. The rear-view TV camera in Brundle's car caught the incident perfectly as the nose of the McLaren suddenly appeared, like a shark in murky waters.

The close season was taken up with arguments over the appeal against Senna's sentence, enlivened by FISA's anger at some of his responses. Eventually, they said that if he did not retract his insults and pay his fine by mid-February, he would lose his Formula One 'superlicence'.

Senna's response, with its combination of icy clarity and bogus humility, must have appealed to the samurai sense of ethics. 'I asked myself about continuing to race,' he said. 'I was perfectly calm and I discussed the matter with Honda and McLaren. I said to them that I was only a driver and that McLaren and Honda would continue after me. I said that I did not want to compromise their efforts and those of the people who work to run the cars. I asked Nobuhiko Kawamoto and Ron Dennis to decide in my place. I said I would completely respect their wishes, that I was ready to retire or fight on as they thought fit.'

Too much was at stake, on all sides. A compromise emerged: Dennis paid the fine, Senna said that he now thought nobody had tried to cheat him out of the title, and Jean-Marie Balestre, the president of FISA, sent him his new licence, along with good wishes for the 1990 season.

Senna turned up at Phoenix looking wan and complaining that the events of the winter had removed his motivation, but he still managed to win, fending off the challenge of a twenty-three-year-old Frenchman of Sicilian descent, Jean Alesi, who had the disrespect, when passed by Senna, to hurl his humble Tyrrell past the world champion at the next corner. It didn't last beyond another few seconds, but nothing like that had happened before. Perhaps the generations were moving on. Senna had turned thirty that month.

His new team mate was Gerhard Berger, who had switched from Ferrari in the hope of challenging Senna on an equal footing. He was soon to learn the truth about that. However much commitment you give, he discovered, Senna will give more. And that is before the question of innate talent comes into the equation.

'Gerhard has difficult times, sure . . . so do I,' Senna said at one point during their collaboration. 'He's very competitive, he tries his maximum all the time. And by using the same equipment together, as we do, you have a very close picture of what the other guy is doing. In such an atmosphere it's so difficult to be friends or even to have respect. It is possible to have respect of each other; we have a good understanding.'

Berger's difficult times included the problem of getting McLaren to construct a car to accommodate his long frame, rather than Senna's shorter build. That took two years, and taught him where the team's priorities were. Later he and Senna became close friends, but not until Berger had got the message from the 'very close picture of what the other guy is doing'. Once he had accepted that what Senna was doing was beyond his own capacity, the friendship could be established – to the point of Senna going along with Berger's practical jokes, such as throwing expensive briefcases out of helicopters or replacing passport photographs with snapshots of gorillas.

There were enough second, third and fourth places for Berger that season to give him fourth place in the final championship table, but there were no wins: the Marlboro McLaren team now belonged to Ayrton Senna, for whom there were further victories in Monaco, Canada, Germany, Belgium and Italy on the way to another showdown with Prost, who himself had won four races in the Ferrari by the time they went back to Suzuka.

At Monza, where Senna and Prost finished first and second, they attended the same post-race press conference and were asked when they might start talking to each other again. Well, Prost said, I offered to shake hands with him at Phoenix, at the beginning of the season. 'I did not think he was sincere about it,' Senna said. 'When he is able to say he is sincere in front of everyone, I will accept it.' And slowly, awkwardly, they did indeed shake hands, to applause from the representatives of the media.

A meaningless response to a meaningless gesture, as it turned out. The tension rose again at Estoril, where Mansell squeezed Prost against the pit wall at the start, and at Jerez, where the Friday afternoon accident to Martin Donnelly shook all the drivers, but none more than Senna. The young Irishman had hit a barrier at almost 150 m.p.h. and as his Lotus disintegrated he was left prone in the middle of the track, with injuries that were to end his Formula One career. The session was halted, and Senna went straight to the place of the accident, where he remained for twenty minutes before locking himself away in the McLaren motorhome. That evening he visited Donnelly in hospital. On the question of danger in motor racing, he had once said: 'It's very strong in my mind. It gives you the right feeling for self-preservation. At moments when you're dealing with danger very near, it's attractive . . . and being attractive, it could go a little bit too far.' Whatever his thoughts as he meditated on Donnelly's accident, the worst he had seen during his time in Formula One so far, at the next race he himself took the danger a little bit too far.

'Not only unsporting, but disgusting,' Alain Prost said after being pushed off the track at something over 130 m.p.h. by Senna at the first corner of the first lap of the Japanese Grand Prix, meaning that the championship race was over and Senna had won his third title while both of them sat stuck in the sand-trap. Half a lap or so from where Senna had seen God two years earlier, now he had executed a truly diabolical manoeuvre. 'He saw I had made a better start,' Prost continued, 'and so he pushed me off. I am not prepared to fight against irresponsible people who are not afraid to die.'

'It was simply two cars trying to make the first corner together,' Senna retorted from behind a façade of implacable calm. 'I had been asking the officials to move pole position to the other side of the track all weekend, and their refusal to do it created so many problems that I suppose this accident was likely to happen. He knew I was going to come down the inside. He made the biggest mistake by closing the door. He knows I always go for the gap. I know what I can do and I am happy inside.'

The depth of feeling against Senna was illustrated in a considered remark by Jackie Stewart, another three-time world champion: 'I don't doubt that Senna always genuinely believes he's in the right, but, well, Hitler believed he was in the right. "I don't run into people," he said. "Come on, Ayrton," I said, "it can't always be the other guy who's at fault . . ." but no, he wouldn't have it. It's a great mistake, deluding yourself.'

Later, we discovered that he hadn't been deluding himself. He'd been lying. But it was possible, as it always is in motor racing, to construct an argument from the other standpoint. Knowing Senna's psychological hold over Prost, it was possible to watch the tape of the rush down to the first right-hand bend and see Prost going slightly wide, perhaps hesitating on the turn-in, possibly even backing off the throttle a fraction as one might, almost subconsciously, if one were preoccupied by what was happening in one's mirrors. Was Senna in fact the casualty of a psyched-out Prost's timidity?

No, not exactly. The point was this, and it did not emerge for more than a year, until Senna had wrapped up his third world championship and was relaxing after the clinching race, again at

Suzuka. He went through the explanation of how, the previous year, the pole position had been switched to the inside of the circuit, off the racing line, where the surface was covered with dust and rubber. Quite reasonably, he asked for it to be changed back to the outside, to restore the pole man's rightful advantage. He thought he had won his case, but it turned out that he had not. The stewards, he claimed, had been overruled by Jean-Marie Balestre, who he believed bore a grudge against him. So then he made his mind up. 'I said to myself, "OK, you try to work cleanly and do the job properly and then you get fucked by certain people. All right, if tomorrow Prost beats me off the line, at the first corner I will go for it . . . and he'd better not turn in because he's not going to make it." And it just happened.'

His phrase of the previous year came back: *someone who shouldn't have been there*. Since he shouldn't have been there, he didn't exist. And if he didn't exist, he can't have been there . . .

When he continued, though, his words made better sense: 'I wish it hadn't happened. We were both off and it was a shit end to the world championship. It was not good for me and not good for Formula One. It was the result of wrong decisions and partiality by the people making them. I won the championship. So what? It was a bad example for everyone.'

'He has completely destroyed everything,' Prost said at the time of the crash. 'Everything that has happened here has shown his real face. For him it is much more important to win the championship than it is for me. It is the only thing he has in life. He is completely screwed up. This man has no value.'

For 1991 Senna would receive $15 million from Marlboro McLaren: almost a million dollars a race, under the terms of a new deal negotiated in many long sessions with Ron Dennis. Plus his personal sponsorship deal with Banco Nacional. Plus many other bits and bobs. He kept his end of the bargain by winning the first four races of the year, including a victory in Brazil, where he finished with only sixth gear left in the MP4/6's gearbox: 'God gave me this race,' he said.

God also let him off, when he had the biggest crash of his career in qualifying for the Mexican Grand Prix. It happened at Peralta, an enormous high-speed banked right-hander that turned through 180 degrees to bring the cars on to the finishing straight. As if Peralta's linear contour were not sufficiently fearsome, it also featured a surface bumpy enough to require the drivers to brace themselves against forces coming from every direction. Oh, and (like Tamburello) practically nothing in the way of a run-off area to allow errant cars to reduce their speed before hitting something solid.

On the Friday, Senna went out and wound himself up for a quick one. Coming into Peralta flat in sixth, he tried to change down to fifth halfway through the bend. The movement, possibly combined with the unevenness of the tarmac, threw the car off balance and off line, and into a spin that took it into the tyre wall on the outside of the track. The McLaren flicked straight over on to its back. Unbelievably, within moments Senna was unclipping his belts, dropping out of the cockpit and walking away unscathed. It was further evidence of the high degree of safety built into modern grand prix cars; after Piquet and Berger at Imola and now Senna in Mexico City, it became harder for those outside the cockpit – officials and spectators – to remember that Formula One was a potentially lethal activity. For drivers too, maybe.

Mexico City, coming during a run of five races without a win, was when he started fretting in private and in public about the amount of power the Honda engines were now delivering, compared with the Ferrari of Prost and, most of all, the new Renault propelling Mansell's and Patrese's Williams. 'Unless we change our own equipment pretty fast,' he predicted, 'we're going to have trouble later in the season.' Honda listened, and worked harder. Senna won in Hungary and Belgium and then picked up enough points to win the title with a second at Suzuka before wrapping up the season with a win at Adelaide. The race in Spain, in which Senna came fifth after a spin, contained an unforgettable sequence in which Senna and Mansell raced wheel to wheel down the long finishing straight at more than 180 m.p.h., Senna on the outside, Mansell challenging, Senna glancing across, sparks flying from the magnesium undertrays, their wheels no more than an inch apart, Mansell looking ahead and taking the corner from Senna with a display of courage and commitment that left the audience breathless and the Brazilian with an enhanced respect for his old adversary.

The second place in Japan, giving him the six points with which he took the title ahead of Mansell, was a contrived and rather unsavoury affair. Berger, without a win in almost two seasons with McLaren (to Senna's dozen in the same period), had led from the start. Senna took over, but then received a radio message from Dennis asking him to let Berger win. So he did, but in the most disingenuous way possible, leading up to the last corner and then slowing dramatically, pulling over to the side, and practically throwing down his cloak for the Austrian to walk over. No one among the watching millions could be in any doubt that this was a gesture *de haut en bas*, publicly expressing a patronizing attitude towards his team-mate (who had, after all, already won five grands prix for Benetton and Ferrari without such assistance).

Old-timers remembered that when Fangio had let Moss win the Englishman's home grand prix in 1955, the maestro had ensured that it looked as though he had been beaten fair and square. Even Moss was not sure. If you had to lose a race as a gesture of fraternity, that was the way to do it. That was sportsmanship – or an older version of it, at any rate.

Amazingly, the friendship between Senna and Berger survived, as – for one more season – did Berger's tenure with McLaren.

Senna's revelations at the Suzuka press conference were sparked off by the replacement of Balestre at the head of the international automobile federation by Max Mosley, an English lawyer (and son of Sir Oswald Mosley) who had worked closely with Bernie Eccle-stone for many years. Historically, Senna had seen Balestre as pro-Prost; now, in a lengthy outburst laced (unusually for him) with emphatic obscenities, he got his complaints off his chest. A few days later, after consultations with Mosley, he issued a state-ment claiming that his remarks, clearly heard and tape-recorded or written down by a roomful of experienced reporters, had been 'misinterpreted'. When I use a word, as Humpty Dumpty said to Alice, it means exactly what I want it to mean: Lewis Carroll would have had fun with the systematic use of doublespeak in the Formula One paddock.

But 1992 was a year of increasing desperation for Senna. Not only had Honda fallen behind in the power race, but the MP4/7 could not match the new Williams. Patrick Head's FW14B made devastatingly effective use of the new technology of computer-controlled active suspension to smooth the passage of the car around the circuit, adjusting its balance and attitude to maximize the efficiency of the aerodynamics. This produced the downforce which allowed the driver to brake later on the entrance to a corner and to floor the throttle earlier and more positively on the exit. It was Williams's year, and Nigel Mansell's: when the first three races ended in one-twos for Williams, with Patrese faithfully shadowing his team leader, Senna knew he was in for a season of trial.

Ominously, too, there was another car and driver apparently able to make a stronger challenge to Williams than Senna and McLaren could muster. The combination of the Benetton B192 and Michael Schumacher was clearly the best of the rest. A year before, aged twenty-two, Schumacher had made a blazing début when he stepped into the humble Jordan and put it into seventh spot on the grid at Spa. Now a string of seconds and thirds culmi-nated in a brilliant victory on his return to Spa in only his eighteenth grand prix. What was more, the nature of the win, earned not just by speed but by tactical intelligence and panache, invited a clear comparison with Senna himself.

Even before that, Schumacher had earned a chance to compare himself with the presiding genius. At Interlagos, on Senna's home turf, they were trailing the Williams pair when Schumacher took advantage of a misfire in the McLaren's Honda engine to pass the world champion on the outside of the uphill left-hand bend leading to the finishing straight. The way Senna muscled back past him on the entrance to the next bend later drew a disgusted response from the German, almost ten years his junior. 'I was quicker than him,' Schumacher said, 'but he was playing some kind of game, which surprised me. I wouldn't have expected this kind of driving from a three-times world champion.'

Senna won at Monaco again, fighting off a charging Mansell in a torrid last lap which saw the Brazilian taking occupation of the road-width to the very limit of acceptability, the two cars finishing with 0.21 sec. between them. (Mansell, who could see the title coming up for him six months away, accepted the nature of his first defeat of the season with good grace.)

Senna won in Hungary, too, which for the sake of decency towards his team he probably had to do, since he had announced to the world before the race, via the BBC's James Hunt, that he had offered his services to Frank Williams next season for nothing. Not a penny. Never mind a million dollars a race. Never mind a million pounds a race, which is what Senna claimed Mansell was demanding for his services at Williams in 1993. Through Hunt, he told Williams and the world that he would drive for a million pounds a race less than Mansell. That was the measure of how badly Ayrton Senna hated not having the best equipment. Banco Nacional would have been happy to make sure that his income did not fall below that of the average São Paulo *favela*-dweller. But the fourth title was what counted.

Mansell was world champion by mid-August, and Senna was on the phone to Frank Williams once, twice, three times a week, trying to persuade him, trying to put together a deal that would get him into the Williams-Renault in time for the next season.

Three wins and fourth place in the world championship table were not what he was all about. 'I am not designed to be second or third,' he had once said. 'I am designed to win.'

The problem was Prost, who had taken 1992 off after falling out with Ferrari and being sacked from the team before the end of the 1991 season. He spent the year talking to Renault, his old employers, and it was at their behest (and expense) that Williams signed the Frenchman. Mansell was world champion, and the British public wanted him to stay with the top British team. But he had no desire to share another motorhome with Prost, whom he considered to have queered his pitch at Ferrari by ensuring that the cars were developed to suit the Frenchman's conservative driving style at the expense of his own more flamboyant, combative approach. For all his popularity with the Italian fans, Mansell never commanded the political skills necessary to survive in the intrigue-riddled atmosphere of Maranello; Prost, by contrast, would have been at home as a Papal *consigliere* of the sixteenth century.

Williams, Senna's long-time admirer, would far rather have had the Brazilian in one of his cars than either of the other drivers; but he was committed to Prost, at Renault's bidding, and Prost would not have Senna. Senna, naturally, felt he had nothing to fear from Prost in equal equipment, which enabled him to issue lofty dismissals of the Frenchman's attitude to the threat of competition.

'If Prost wants to come back and win another title, he should be sportive,' Senna said at the press conference after the race at Estoril, with Mansell and Berger at his side. 'The way he is doing it, he is behaving like a coward. He must be prepared to race anybody in any conditions, on equal terms, and not the way he wants to win the championship. It's like if you go into a 100-metre sprint and you want to have running shoes and everybody else should have lead shoes. That's the way he wants to race. That is not racing.' The change in his peers' attitude towards Prost over the years could be measured in the broad smiles of Mansell and Berger.

On the other hand, somebody like Derek Warwick, whose

potential as a grand prix winner was probably wrecked by Senna's veto in 1986, must have felt sick when he heard the stuff about being 'prepared to race anybody in any conditions, on equal terms'. But Senna was right: a true champion must fight for everything, just as he always had. Not merely for the first corner, or the finish line. For the best car, the best contract, the best conditions. When he insulted Prost in that way, when he became the first world champion ever to accuse another of cowardice, Senna was actually paying his opponent the highest compliment: he was fighting him with every weapon he could find, even handfuls of mud from the gutter.

Prost saw Mansell off easily enough in the battle for a Williams seat. The team bosses, never enamoured of the Englishman's endless complaining and his readiness to transfer the blame for failure, found it relatively easy to decline the opportunity to boost his bank balance by another $16 million or so. In their terms, that was $16 million that could be spent on research and development, on new wind-tunnel facilities and exotic metals and the salaries of a few more software programmers. Mansell left for America, where he would win the Indycar series at his first attempt – and, for that historic deed, earn no more than a fraction of the sum he had demanded from Williams. Instead the team promoted Damon Hill, who had performed well as their test driver in the previous year. Hill cost practically nothing, and he never complained about a thing.

Then Prost almost did Senna's job for him. An outspoken interview in a French newspaper, in which he criticized the activities of the governing body over the preceding seasons, brought down wrath and the threat of a disciplinary hearing that could lead to suspension. 'I'd be surprised if serious action wasn't taken against Prost,' Bernie Ecclestone said. 'One race? Two races? I don't know.' Frank Williams was equally pessimistic: 'I fear he could be out for two or three races. But I hope that reason will win the day.' Prost himself told a French reporter: 'I don't want a polemic. The only thing I can say is that I don't see why I should be punished. Other people have done worse things. What's more, FISA have read what was in the press, but they have not heard a cassette recording of this famous interview. I will make the World Council listen to it. And I'm not worried. But if ever I get sanctioned, I will stop racing.'

Senna sat back and licked his lips, hopeful that Prost had signed his own expulsion order. Refusing to put his name to a new contract with McLaren, Senna accepted an offer from Emerson Fittipaldi and Roger Penske to try an Indy car at Phoenix's Firebird Raceway, which led to rumours that he might be following Mansell into American racing. But he was just teasing, really. He kept the line open to Frank Williams, and he kept Ron Dennis waiting, and he prepared himself to play the long game.

With his appearance before the World Council pending, Prost arrived at Kyalami in time to join Hill at a pre-race photocall on the grid, posing on either side of one of the team's new sponsors: Sonic the Hedgehog, a giant blue cartoon creature whose image had been painted overnight on the flanks of the Williams FW15s. Maybe Nuvolari and Fangio would have gone along with such a scheme; maybe not.

Ron Dennis, interestingly, was said to have turned down the Sonic sponsorship because he didn't fancy the idea of seeing a blue hedgehog painted on the side of his cars. Dennis's enthusiasm for clean lines and crisp edges is a keynote of his team, whose devotion to neatness is so obsessive that the cutting up of the coloured tape for the pit-stop markings on the pits apron is performed not with a pair of scissors or a Stanley knife but a surgeon's scalpel.

Senna was in the McLaren pit at South Africa, too, turning up at the last minute to take the wheel of the new Ford-powered MP4/8, which he had tested briefly at Silverstone. So late had he left his decision that Dennis found himself with three drivers for two cars: he had hired Michael Andretti, son of the former world champion Mario Andretti; and then, still fearing Senna's defection to Williams, he had brought in Mika Hakkinen, a fast young Finn, from Lotus. Dennis called a press conference at Kyalami to explain what was going on. Senna and Andretti would start the season, he said, but Senna was working on a race to race basis, and Hakkinen would be held in reserve.

Senna used the event to launch his offensive against Ford, who were supplying McLaren with last year's engines, having made a deal with Benetton as their major clients. 'Ultimately the engine doesn't have the power that you need if you really want to win,' he said. 'We know they have a better engine because our engine here is two steps down from Benetton's. I hope the team can have that as soon as possible. That will help not only the team but Formula One, which needs urgently to improve the show. For the remainder of the season, it's not only my personal desire but the goal of the team that we should continue. But this decision isn't only for one person.'

The belief in the paddock was that McLaren now had a 'thinking' gearbox, programmed to every corner of a particular circuit, making the gear-changing decisions for the driver and allowing him to concentrate on steering, accelerating and braking. The real bonus would be that, in combination with active suspension, the new transmission would keep the car smooth and efficient.

Senna was fascinated by these developments, but as a racing driver he did not welcome them because he knew that they tended to 'level up' the abilities of the drivers as well as increase the costs of development and manufacture. 'The machines have taken away the character,' he had said the previous year, 'and it is the character that the sponsors and public are looking for. At the top, you have a few characters of conflicting personality; the rest, without good results, don't have any credibility. We must reduce costs so that we return to an era when the emphasis is on people, not computers.' He wanted to be challenged by his own limits, 'and by someone who is born of the same skin and bone and where the difference is between brain and experience and adaptation to the course. I do not want to be challenged by someone else's computer. If I give 100 per cent to my driving, which is my hobby

111

as well as my profession, I can compete with anyone, but not computers.'

Where McLaren's technology could help was over the question of the Ford engine's power deficiency, some 80 horsepower down on the Renault's. But the electronic throttle and automatic gearbox could help Senna get off the line at Kyalami. 'I'd like to be the first into the first corner, that's for sure,' he said. 'After the start, I'll tell you how clever is my computer.'

And sure enough as Prost, the poleman, bogged down when the green light came on, Senna leapt into the lead. Suddenly all pre-season doubts about his motivation were shown to be nonsense. He was in a racing car, and instinct had taken over. The strength of his desire was apparent as soon as Prost gathered himself together for a challenge. Once Prost had got past the second-placed Schumacher, he spent a dozen bloodcurdling laps trying to find a way past Senna's full repertoire of feints, dives and outright blocks, some of them executed with a brutal finality that suggested he knew exactly how much humiliation Prost was prepared to take. But after a year out of the cockpit, Prost stuck doggedly to the daunting task and at last, holding his breath and probably closing his eyes, squeezed by into a lead that he held until the end, eventually extending the gap to more than a minute.

With four laps to go, however, the light had turned strange and silvery and suddenly there were big drops of rain on the hospitality box windows. With two laps left, a loud crack announced the opening of the heavens over the back of the circuit. Immediately, the rain mixed with the fine red dust of the high veldt to produce a surface on which cars started falling off all over the place. With a lap to go, Prost crossed the finishing line almost at a crawl, waving his arm: stop it now!

At the winner's press conference, Prost explained his problems at the start with the car's clutch and mentioned that he had the wrong pressure in his first set of tyres, that the front end of the car wasn't working properly, and that he had finished the race with a broken seat. Then he started to talk about the weather, and about the new rule stipulating that, in the event of rain, a race should not be stopped 'unless the circuit is blocked or it is dangerous to continue'.

'It was very slippery towards the end, with two laps to go,' he said. 'One more lap and it would have been very difficult. I think it would have been better to stop it with two laps to go. Nobody's going to stop for rain tyres at that stage. I think for the future we should know that.'

The microphone was handed to Senna. Did the rainmaster agree? He sat silently, and the longer he sat, the more certain we became that something good was coming.

'Yes and no,' he said finally, and the room hummed with gleeful anticipation of another chapter to add to the long rivalry. 'For safety reasons, yes, we should stop. But for competitive reasons, no, because the race has a number of laps and a distance to be covered, and it's the same for everybody. It's a question of whether to stop and put wet tyres on to come across the finish line or take a gamble and not stop and maybe not come around. It's a situation which makes life extremely difficult, but it comes down also to each individual to make a decision. If you just think about safety, sure, stop the race. But we know the rules, and they are made not to stop . . . you can stop, if you like, but you just don't if you don't. So it's a question of point of view.'

On the face of it, a civilized disagreement between profession- als. Not a voice raised. No hard looks exchanged. But the sub-text! *If you just think about safety, sure, stop the race.* Nothing could have been more carefully calculated to insult Prost, to evoke memories of the battles he had lost to Senna in the past, and by implication to devalue a victory which, in any case, as Senna went on to reveal, had been earned only because his own McLaren had suffered from a problem with the active suspension.

'The car was impossible,' Senna said in that soft, thoughtful tone. 'It was a shame. In the warm-up it was fine. One corner of

113

the car went completely out of my control. I thought it might be a puncture, but then I realized it was an electronic problem. It was hell to drive the car. Immediately Schumacher caught me up, and then Alain, and they were much quicker than me – not just round the corners but on the straights. But, given the car we have, it's a good result.'

A check of the lap times proved that Senna's tale was not just part of another Formula One mind game. His times had risen exactly when he said they had, down to a small blip when he tried to give his tyres a rest as early as the third lap. He had given us the sort of accurate analysis his engineers were accustomed to hearing.

The winner, sitting next to him, looked increasingly bleak. We thought we had witnessed the return of Alain Prost, champion racing driver. Now we weren't so sure.

Later that week Prost put on his best suit to appear before the international federation's World Council in Paris. He played his tape, spoke his words of reason, and made his peace. He was on the way to his fourth world title.

And yet, in finishing the 1993 season as runner-up to the principal rival of his career, Senna – the man who said, 'I am not designed to come second or third' – perhaps put together the most impressive year of all. In the MP4/8, he discovered a car that ran out of breath on the straights but could be thrown into the corners like a Formula Ford. There was only one pole position for him in the entire season, but time and again the crowds could watch the nose of the red and white car twitching as he searched for the limit of adhesion, just the way Peterson and Villeneuve used to do. His reward at the beginning of the season, while Prost was still rediscovering his competitive edge and getting to grips with the new Williams technology, came with wins at Interlagos and Donington.

There were other bonuses to these victories besides cups and cheques. At a sponsors' party at Interlagos he met Adriane Galisteu, a twenty-year-old blonde from Lapa, a working-class suburb of

São Paulo. She and nine other girls had been sent by the Elite model agency to earn $1,000 a day handing round canapés and smiling at the guests in the Shell VIP tent. They met again at Senna's victory celebration party, held at the Limelight disco in São Paulo. Shortly thereafter she was discovering that the bedroom closet at his holiday home in Angra dos Reis held forty or fifty pairs of identical white tennis shoes. They were to spend the remainder of his life together: 405 days, by her count.

A lesser perk came in the form of having fun at his chief rival's expense, lightening the mood of their vendetta although never relieving the pressure on an increasingly fretful Prost. After all, if your enemy is laughing at you, you start to wonder if your flies are undone. In the aftermath of the majestic victory at Donington, for example, Senna transformed the post-race press conference with a single moment of expert comic timing.

He was late into the room, delayed by an informal celebration of a performance he knew ranked with any he had ever given. When he arrived, Prost was explaining all the things that had gone wrong during the course of what was for him a tactically disastrous race hindered by no fewer than seven panicky pit stops. It was the usual mundane parade of racing drivers' excuses, multiplied by about three. The gearbox hadn't worked properly, that was the first thing. There was still a problem with the clutch. The tyre pressures hadn't been right, the aerodynamics were all over the place, the sun-roof had rusted up, the ashtray was full and the French tax laws were murderous. At that point you wouldn't have bet on the triple world champion getting a Volvo estate out of the Donington car park in one piece.

Senna leaned forward, towards the microphone.

'Why,' he said quietly, 'don't you change cars with me?'

It was the only dry moment of the day, and it brought the house down.

At Imola, Prost began the run of wins that took him to the title, interrupted by Senna's inevitable victory at Monaco: his sixth, a record. Prost was crowned at Estoril, after which he announced his retirement at the end of the season. 'The sport has given me a lot,' he said, 'but I decided that the game wasn't worth it any more. I have taken too many blows.' To no one's surprise, Frank Williams told the world that Ayrton Senna would be driving one of his cars in 1994. The Brazilian's two-year campaign had finally paid off.

The pressure gone, Senna wrapped up the season with wins at Suzuka and Adelaide, his thirty-fourth and thirty-fifth over the six seasons in the cockpit of a McLaren. The Japanese race produced the only physical altercation of Senna's season when, irritated by what he considered to be the disrespectful tactics employed by the Jordan driver Eddie Irvine, he went to seek him out in the Irish team's motorhome to administer a ticking-off. Afterwards it emerged that Senna's friend Berger had wound him up, pouring a couple of celebratory glasses of schnapps into a man who seldom touched alcohol; at any rate it was enough to enable Irvine's studied show of dumb insolence to goad the head boy into turning back as he was leaving, and giving the cheeky third-former a cuff on the head. Ill-advised, in the modern world, but you couldn't blame him.

Still, for a season that had promised nothing once Prost removed the immediate possibility of a transfer to Williams, things had not worked out too badly at all.

Chapter Eight

Senna and Adriane seemed settled, which may be a strange way to describe people who were constantly on the move, using private jets, helicopters and limousines to ferry them between the house on the Algarve at Quinta do Lago, the Rio beach house at Angra dos Reis, the São Paulo apartment on the Rua Paraguai and the da Silva family farm at Tatui.

'I felt that, with Adriane Galisteu, Ayrton was having luck in life,' Emerson Fittipaldi wrote after his death. 'He had found his other half, and his maturity as a human being was visible.'

While Senna was alive, the discrepancy between his social background and that of Adriane, brought up by her mother in considerably less privileged circumstances, was allowed to carry no significance. When he was away, testing a car or fulfilling a sponsor's requirements, Adriane took lessons in English, the lingua franca of the paddock, and jogged under the supervision of Nuno Cobra so that she would be able to run in the mornings with Ayrton, whose devotion to his physical fitness regime was absolute.

Cobra was a close friend of long standing, and something of a personal philosopher. 'Life is passing you by,' Adriane heard him telling Senna during the early weeks of 1994, as they trained on the running track of the University of São Paulo. 'Seize it.'

In January Senna went to Estoril to try an updated version of last year's Williams; the new FW16 would not be ready until the early days of March, three weeks before the first race of the season. In between there was plenty of opportunity to play on the jet-skis at Angra and the kart track at Tatui with his nieces Bia and Paulinha and his nephew Bruno, the children of Viviane and her husband, Flávio Lalli.

And there was time, too, for business matters, which were assuming a larger role in his life. 'I am trying to find new activities, a source of motivation for when I've finished,' he said. 'I believe I will be able to find some real alternatives in business.' In 1993, his million-dollars-a-race deal had led *Forbes* magazine to rank him third in their annual list of the highest-earning sports people. His off-track income, from Banco Nacional, other endorsements and his own ventures, would probably have doubled that. A videogame under his name sold 800,000 copies, for example; there was a range of leisure clothing. Now he moved into a higher gear, announcing that his company Senna Import was the new distributor of Audi cars in Brazil. Cavaro, an Italian bicycle manufacturer, launched a new carbon-fibre mountain bike bearing his name. There were collaborations with TAG-Heuer watches, Mont Blanc pens and Ducati motorcycles. And, closest to his heart, there was the launch of *Senninha e sua turma* (Senninha and his gang), a witty and well-drawn fortnightly children's cartoon magazine devoted to the adventures of a boy racing driver bearing a close resemblance to Brazil's real-life hero. Senninha also jet-skied, outwitted baddies, and, in edition number four, fell in love with a little blonde girl. The magazine, Senna said, was an expression of his desire to give something back to children; he had plans to direct the profits from some of these ventures into projects to help the street kids of São Paulo. In March he donated $45,000 to a charity for sick children at the behest of his old friend Professor Sid Watkins, the Formula One circus's resident medical officer.

But when he sat in the new car for the first time during a test at Paul Ricard in February, he discovered something that disturbed him: the 1994 Williams did not have the inherent superiority enjoyed by its predecessors, and which had persuaded him to make such strenuous and protracted efforts to join the team. It was uncomfortably small in the cockpit, its handling was disconcertingly difficult to predict, and, as testing at Imola revealed, it was not as quick as Michael Schumacher's new Benetton.

In 1992 and 1993, the combination of Patrick Head's chassis, Adrian Newey's aerodynamics and Bernard Dudot's Renault engine had given Mansell and Prost what was practically a magic carpet. But their domination, and the costly spread of computer technology throughout Formula One, had led the FIA to bring in new regulations for 1994, banning the sort of devices that were horribly expensive, even by Formula One's inflated standards, and were also perceived to reduce the driver's contribution, thereby diminishing the sport as a human spectacle. So out went fully automatic gearboxes (including McLaren's programmed job and Williams's projected constantly variable transmission); out went the device called traction control, which matched engine revs to road speed and eliminated wheel spin, at great cost to the spectacle since almost any idiot could floor the throttle and turn the wheel; most crucially for Williams, out went the enormously complicated active suspension, which they had perfected while others struggled. There was the added complication of reduced petrol tankage, brought in to create a need for refuelling stops in order to increase the entertainment value for television: an idiotically irresponsible measure.

The new Williams was technically a more straightforward car, but it is in the nature of racing-car designers always to explore new solutions, and no solution to the problems set by a modern Formula One car can ever be called simple. From the day it first turned a wheel, the FW16 had its drivers and engineers worried.

Schumacher, by contrast, looked and sounded highly confident at Silverstone in mid-March, doing the final fettling work on his Benetton ten days before the opening round in Brazil. But he was not silly enough to overplay it when told that people were speculating about how he was now faster than Senna. 'It's nice to know people have that trust in me,' he said mildly as a bright spring sun chased thunderclouds across the sky outside the Benetton motorhome and the yawp of a lone Tyrrell floated across the infield. 'The only thing I can say is that I've got another year of experience. Hopefully we can push the Williams, sometimes stay close, sometimes win a race, but as for the championship, I think we're still one more step away from that.'

Senna and Hill, he said, had 'the best package' for the season. 'But that doesn't mean that in some races where they don't find the right set-up, we might find a very good set-up – and we'll be very close, we'll fight together, and then by strategies or stuff we're going to win races. But too many bad things would need to happen to other teams for us really to have the chance to win the championship. Drivers like Senna or Hill, a team like Williams . . . they don't make mistakes.'

His team were helpful to a lone observer that day, but when they were asked about the function of the three coloured buttons on the centre of the Benetton's steering wheel, they clammed up in unison. It was curious, but it didn't seem very important at the time.

A few days later Williams held a final test at Silverstone, and invited the media. Damon Hill, under pressure from the British newspapers to match the exploits of the departed Nigel Mansell, told the journalists that he had no intention of becoming another victim of what he called 'Sennaphobia': a clever description of the point at which respect for the maestro shaded into fear, inhibiting aggression. Hill had read his history books, and knew what had become of Cecotto, De Angelis, Dumfries and Michael Andretti, and how even Prost and Berger had been made to suffer. His team mate, he said, was just another racing driver, albeit a great one.

Senna went to Interlagos ready to celebrate the tenth anniversary of his arrival in Formula One, unsure of what was in store. 'The cars are very fast and difficult to drive,' he said. 'It's going to be a season with lots of accidents, and I'll risk saying we'll be lucky if something really serious doesn't happen.' It would be a more open championship this year, he added; he would have said that anyway, but this time he meant it.

At a post-qualifying press conference organized by Renault, just after wrapping up pole position a third of a second ahead of

Schumacher, he shared the platform with Patrick Faure, the president of the French company's sporting division, and launched straightaway into one of his sermons on the need to fight complacency. 'We've seen today the gap being almost insignificant between our car and Schumacher's,' he said. Then he drew a deep breath, and turned towards Faure. 'As far as the future season is concerned, it all depends on the development programme that both Williams-Renault and Benetton-Ford can do. I hope Mr Faure will keep on pushing the technicians from Renault to ensure that they continue the development of the engine, and also push Frank Williams and Patrick Head and all the engineers to get the new modifications in the development of the chassis.' This, the sort of self-criticism normally confined to a locked motorhome or a debugged boardroom, was uttered before a single lap of the season had been run. It was in some respects a familiar gambit, and in the past an effective one. Renault and Williams were being put on notice that, notwithstanding their two consecutive championships with Mansell and Prost, they must now prepare themselves to deal with not merely different circumstances but also the requirements of an altogether more exigent character. Nothing less would do, he was saying, than total commitment.

What particularly concerned Senna was the car's response to bumps, combined with its reluctance to hold its line on low-speed corners. Interlagos is a circuit with an abrasive, uneven surface, compared to the billiard-table tarmac of most grand prix tracks, and without its computer-driven electronic ride system the Williams was reacting badly. According to Hill's post-season assessment, at this stage the car was 'virtually undrivable' in the slow corners. 'And in the quick ones it threatened to turf you off the track at any moment,' he added, pointing out that the problem was compounded by the narrowness of the footwell, which impeded the transfer of the right foot from accelerator pedal to brake.

Senna, anxious to disguise these problems from his rivals' attention and to get on with stamping his authority on the season, took the lead from the start on Sunday afternoon, and built a small cushion while Schumacher was finding a way past Alesi's Ferrari. By the time they made their first pit stops, however, Schumacher was only a second behind, and good work by the Benetton crew allowed him to leave the pits in a narrow lead which he soon extended to five seconds and then, after the second set of stops, to nine seconds. Senna had seemed powerless to do anything about it, but with twenty-five laps to go he launched an assault. Gradually the gap came down: 9.2 sec., 8.1, 6.3, 5.5, 6.2, 6.0, 5.0. But on the next time round, lap fifty-six, with fifteen left to run, he was coming out of Cotovello, a slowish uphill ninety-degree left-hander, when he put the power on in third gear and the back end of the car stepped out of line, snapping him into a halfspin. As the Williams came to a stop in mid-track, the engine stalled. Around the circuit, his home crowd looked on, appalled, cheated of the denouement they had been counting on. Senna popped his belts and stepped out, leaving the victory to Schumacher. On the TV monitors, an unsentimental readout told us that at the moment the spin started his heart had been beating at a rate of 164 per minute.

It looked like the most banal sort of error, something a beginner might do, or a driver from a lower formula experiencing the power of a Formula One car for the first time, not a triple world champion. Nevertheless he tried to take the blame. 'There was nothing wrong with the car,' he admitted. 'It was my fault. I was pushing too hard.' In the motorhome his words carried a different message, one conveyed to Didcot, where the Williams engineers continued to wrestle with the problem. Both he and Hill, who finished a struggling second to the elated Schumacher, needed the attentions of Josef Leberer, Senna's travelling masseur and reflexologist, to ease away the strain of battling against their own cars' evil tendencies.

Now they were paying for the late delivery of the FW16, for allowing Benetton precious extra weeks in which to test and refine the B194. But Senna had his suspicions that there was more to it than that. And at the second race, the Pacific Grand Prix on the new Aida circuit near Osaka in Japan, his thoughts darkened further. He took pole by a fifth of a second from Schumacher, but in the Saturday morning warm-up both he and Hill spun their cars at the same corner. In the paddock on race day, Senna lay on the floor of the Williams cabin for an hour, clearing his thoughts. His race, however, lasted only a few seconds. Schumacher got the better start, and led into the first corner. Behind him, Senna felt the impact of Hakkinen's nose on his own gearbox. The Williams slewed sideways, presenting a wide target which was duly hit by Nicola Larini's Ferrari, both of them ending up in the sand as Schumacher raced on to victory. Afterwards Senna stood and watched the two Benettons, noting the differences in the behaviour of the car of Schumacher and the apparently identical but much slower one of his young Dutch team mate, Jos Verstappen.

Trailing Schumacher in the championship by twenty points to nil, Senna pushed the team even harder. By comparison with the Benetton, the FW16 lacked grip in slow corners, its front wing was inefficient, and the way the air flowed beneath its body made it over-sensitive to changes in pitch (the fore-and-aft shifts of balance caused by accelerating and braking). It was a twitchy car, not trustworthy; 'horrible', in Hill's word. Not, in fact, the kind of car to be taken by the scruff of its neck and overdriven in the manner of which Senna had shown his mastery the previous season with the underpowered but high-spirited and responsive MP4/8. But even this, in Senna's eyes, didn't quite explain the success of Schumacher and the Benetton, on the face of it nothing more than an exceptionally gifted and ambitious young pilot at the wheel of a carefully developed but perfectly standard combination of machinery (with a Ford engine certifiably less powerful than the Renault). That, Senna felt, shouldn't have been enough.

All through the early weeks of the season there had been fears that someone would find a way of circumventing the new regulations, which had been devised to close up the performance gaps between the cars and put the racing back in the hands of the drivers.

Before Interlagos, Mosley had threatened 'draconian' punishments: anyone caught cheating would be thrown out of the championship. But finding the limit of the rules is, after all, what racing-car designers are for, and no one was very surprised when Larini's slip of the tongue in Japan led the FIA's technical inspectors to discover some sort of a traction control programme hidden away in the Ferrari's engine management software. What was a surprise, at least to the unworldly, was the reluctance of the authorities to impose the promised sanction. A slap on the wrist was felt to be enough. But then what value would a season without Ferrari have at the box office?

Senna's thoughts were all on the next race, at Imola on 1 May, but ten days earlier he was fulfilling a patriotic duty at the Parc des Princes in Paris, kicking off a friendly soccer match between Brazil and Paris Saint-Germain, the club of Rai de Oliveira and Ricardo Rocha, two members of the Brazilian squad. Wearing a grey jumper and black slacks on a pleasant spring evening, he acknowledged the applause of the massed ranks of the city's Brazilian exiles, all dressed in yellow and green, draped with the *bandeira* and playing samba tunes on drums and pipes. Sadly, their enthusiasm was rewarded with nothing more than a sterile goalless draw and afterwards the Brazilian coach, the endlessly patient Carlos Alberto Parreira, was pinned to the wall of the dressing room by the sixty-odd football reporters who had followed him across the Atlantic and now were keen to know, on behalf of the 150 million experts back home, how on earth he expected to win the World Cup with that bunch of deadbeats.

Senna slipped away into the night, to a dinner date at La Coupole with his friend António Braga. Both the racing driver and the soccer team were favourites to land a fourth world championship in 1994, and both were in trouble.

When he arrived at Imola by helicopter on the afternoon of the following Thursday, 28 April, it was to discover that Head, Newey and the Williams technicians had been hard at work. The front wheels had been moved back, as had the front wing, which had also been raised. Together, these changes improved the aerodynamic balance, although developments later in the season showed that there was still plenty wrong with the behaviour of the Williams at this stage.

The front cover of that week's *Autosport* carried a picture of the Brazilian looking pensive and the banner headline: 'Senna: Can he take the heat?' A tabloid-style simplification, and something of an insult to a triple world champion, but a good indication of the degree to which motor racing, like most other modern sports with a television following, had grown to depend on a constantly rising level of hype. And, after a spin and a crash in two races, a question just about worth asking.

The Williams was a little better as a result of the work at Didcot, and that weekend he set the fastest practice time yet again, his third in three races that season, and the sixty-fifth and last of his career.

On the first day of qualifying his time was half a second faster than Schumacher's, the day disrupted by a spectacular accident to Rubens Barrichello, whose Jordan flew through the air at 146 m.p.h. like a jet fighter before spearing the tyre wall at the Variante Bassa and rolling twice. When the young Brazilian regained consciousness in the pits, Senna was standing over him. Then, having ascertained that his compatriot was not badly injured, he returned to complete the practice session, and to spend most of the afternoon in an intense debriefing session with his race engineer, David Brown.

Some time during the Friday afternoon he saw his pilot, Owen O'Mahony, who had flown him into Forli airport in his $12m eight-seater British Aerospace HS125 jet. O'Mahony was surprised when Senna handed him three signed photographs of himself with O'Mahony. 'I'd never had a picture of the two of us together,' the pilot recalled five days later, as he stood in the arrivals area of São Paulo airport waiting for his employer's coffin to arrive. 'I'd been meaning to ask him for ages. And suddenly, in the middle of a grand prix meeting, he fished around in his briefcase and pulled them out. I don't know why it should have been then.'

On Saturday afternoon, eighteen minutes into the second qualifying session, the Austrian driver Roland Ratzenberger left the track at the Villeneuve kink, possibly as a result of damage sustained to the front wing of his Simtek when he went over a kerb on the previous lap. He was travelling at something approaching 200 m.p.h. when he hit the concrete wall bordering that part of the circuit, and suffered injuries that killed him instantly.

Ratzenberger was the thirty-second driver to be killed in post-war Formula One, but he was also the first fatality in twelve years, since Ricardo Paletti had died after driving straight into the back of another car on the grid at Montreal in 1982. That made Ratzenberger's death all the more resonant to a generation of drivers who had never experienced such a loss, at least at that level. (By contrast, during Stirling Moss's time in Formula One, from 1954 to 1961, seven drivers were killed at grand prix meetings.) Senna was particularly deeply affected, and when the session had been halted he commandeered a safety car to take him to the scene, where he examined the track and the wreckage before returning to the pits. There he was reprimanded by the race director, John Corsmit, for taking the car without asking permission. Corsmit was right, at least by the book: the car might have been needed elsewhere. But Senna's mind was on other imperatives, and there was a lengthy argument. 'At least someone is concerned about safety,' he shouted at Corsmit. Those who were around Senna that afternoon remember a look they hadn't seen in his face before; not surprising, since it was the first time he had needed to face up to the implications of the death of a Formula One colleague.

That night, at his hotel in Castel San Pietro, ten kilometres from Imola, he called Adriane twice, either side of dinner. She had arrived from Brazil at their home in the Algarve the previous day. In the first call, he told her that he didn't want to race the next day. He had never said such a thing to her before. He was crying.

Later, after a meal with friends and a conversation with Frank Williams, who was staying in the same hotel, he called her again, and this time his voice was calmer and his attitude different. It was OK now, he said. He was going to race. His last words to her: 'Come and pick me up at Faro airport at eight-thirty tomorrow night. I can't wait to see you.'

The mellower mood was still in evidence the next morning, race day, when he was fastest in the warm-up session and then recorded a lap for the French television station TF1, for which Prost was providing commentary. Over the in-car radio link, Senna sent a greeting: 'I would like to say welcome to my old friend, Alain Prost. Tell him we miss him very much.' Later, he and Prost talked warmly in the paddock. 'I miss you,' Senna repeated to the rival who no longer represented a threat.

Senna and Berger had talked with Niki Lauda, now a special consultant to Ferrari, about the accidents and the issues they raised. They discussed the idea of holding a meeting at Monaco, the next race, to revive the old concept of the Grand Prix Drivers' Association, a body set up in the mid-sixties at the instigation of Jo Bonnier, and whose initiatives had improved the security of circuits and cars in a relatively primitive era before withering during the eighties, partly as a result of its own success in reducing the level of danger. Later in the morning, at the regular pre-race drivers' briefing, they stood and observed a minute's silence for Ratzenberger. Acting at Senna's behest, Berger raised a reservation about the use of a safety car, to be brought on to the circuit after accidents to pace the field until the track was clear. They were worried that making the cars hold station at low speed would allow their tyres to cool down, making them inefficient and possibly dangerous in the moments after racing resumed. Senna added a few words. He, Berger and Schumacher left the meeting deep in conversation.

Race time. And a few good examples of how a death does funny things to the memories of witnesses. Someone says that they saw

Senna walking round the back of his car just before the race, looking at it suspiciously. Someone else, who knew him as well as
anybody outside his family, says that even the way he pulled on his
fireproof balaclava was different. Another points out, as if it were
deeply significant, that he departed from his usual practice by
taking his helmet off while the car was on the grid before the start
at Imola, something he never did (wrong: he sometimes did).
Damon Hill, on the other hand, says he was in a normal state of
mental preparation for the race: 'totally focused'.

Adriane was watching on TV in Portugal. 'To me,' she wrote
in her awkward but touching memoir, 'at that moment of tense
expression and hands firmly gripping the car, he was just thinking.
For the first time in his career, he felt the fragility of the machine
and the fragility of the human being. A man had just died in front
of him. A friend had hurt himself against the wall. Until then, the
driver Ayrton Senna had sat in his car and driven on the limits.
Suddenly other feelings had interfered in his life: surprise, fear . . .'

A fair guess, from a few hundred miles away. Nothing mysterious or mystical about any of it. But when the race started, the
racing driver took over.

He led from the start, with Schumacher close behind. Before the
field had all crossed the starting line, however, there was chaos.
J. J. Lehto stalled his Benetton, and was hit from behind by Pedro
Lamy. A wheel from Lamy's Lotus was ripped off and flew into
the crowd, injuring eight spectators and a policeman. As the
twenty-four remaining cars howled round the back of the circuit,
John Corsmit sent out the safety car.

This was what Senna and Berger had been anxious about. A
measure borrowed that season from Indycar racing, the safety car's
job is to come in at the head of the field, just in front of the leader,
slowing them down and circulating until crash debris has been
cleared away and spilt oil covered up. In America, it serves the
secondary function of allowing the field to bunch up, artificially

enhancing the excitement. There is little doubt that this was in the minds of Mosley and Ecclestone when the FIA adopted the idea. Terrified of the danger of falling ratings after years of processional racing during the McLaren and Williams eras, they were looking for anything that might boost the thrill factor. Refuelling stops were one notion, only a decade after they had been banned on safety grounds; the safety car was another. But what worried Senna and Berger was that when the cars' tyres cooled down, the lack of heat would lower the pressure inside the tyre, the rubber would contract, and the tyres' diameter would be reduced. In cars running with a ground clearance so finely adjusted that a couple of millimetres could ruin the handling, this might be a critical factor.

For five laps, Senna trailed round behind the black saloon, Schumacher and the rest droning along in his wake. Out on the start line, course marshals worked fast to clear the debris from the cars of Lamy and Lehto. Then, with the field approaching the finishing straight at the end of the fifth lap, the safety car peeled off into the pit lane, releasing the racers to resume their combat.

As they entered Tamburello, the flat-out left-hander after the pits, Schumacher noticed that Senna was taking a tight line, the car jiggling on the bumps, sparks coming up from the magnesium skid-plates under the car. Nothing particularly extraordinary about that, although later it emerged that Senna had warned Hill of the bumps at Tamburello, telling him to stay wide.

They crossed the line at the end of lap six with Senna still in the lead, Schumacher close behind, Hill already five seconds further back, his car feeling twitchy on its cold tyres.

Schumacher with two wins and twenty points, Senna with nothing. People talking about Schumacher as the new Senna, maybe even faster and fitter than the old one. Ten years younger, for sure. Adriane knew Ayrton took him seriously, because of the way he referred to him only as 'the German', in the way he had spoken of Prost as 'the Frenchman' during their years of poisoned rivalry.

'Our season starts here,' Senna had told a television reporter before the race. Now, at 190 m.p.h. he went into Tamburello for the seventh time.

Frank Williams watched it from the TV monitor in the Williams pit. A helicopter-borne camera focused on the wreckage, as orange-overalled marshals fussed around the yellow helmet. Alone in all the world, the camera held an unflinching gaze.

'Three minutes . . . five minutes . . .' In his office at the Didcot factory many months later, strapped to the standing frame which he sometimes uses instead of a wheelchair, Williams recalled how it had seemed to last for ever. 'Those good old Italian TV cameras never left him alone.' A laugh with all the humour erased, a flash of his startling jade eyes. 'Television is a major reason for the sport's success, but it's also a problem we have to face. When Ayrton was killed, it was immensely public. Terrible. But we can't have it all ways.'

Even when eighty people died at Le Mans in 1955, the race went on. It always has. Damon Hill had to drive past the accident as it was happening, knowing that it was Senna, knowing that it was a big one, not knowing whether he was alive or dead.

I thought of something Phil Hill, the first American world champion, had said in the early sixties, when he drove his Ferrari past the scene of a bad accident involving a team-mate: 'What did it do to me? Nothing. Do I sound callous? I used to go to pieces. I'd see an accident like that and feel so weak inside that I wanted to quit, to stop the car and get out. I could hardly make myself go past it. But I'm older now. When I see something horrible I put my foot down, because I know everyone else is lifting his.'

In the case of Senna's accident, it was different. The red flags came out as the cars went through the Acque Minerali turn on the back leg of the circuit. They slowed, and Schumacher brought them to a halt at the entrance to the pit lane. Had they been told of Senna's death then, probably none of them would have wanted to resume. Senna's death was of another order. He was the best of them, and they thought him indestructible. Later, most of them would have the same response: if it could happen to him, it could happen to me. But, waiting in the pit lane for the instruction to go out and form up for the restart, they didn't know.

They didn't know because it hadn't been certified on the spot. If it had, the Italian police would have taken charge and begun their investigations, questioning witnesses, impounding equipment and preventing the race taking place. Remember: 'Television is a major reason for the sport's success . . .'

Senna's body was lifted from the crumpled Williams and laid on the ground, where Professor Watkins and his crew went through the motions of a tracheotomy to clear his airways, and cardiac massage to revive him. He was still officially alive when he was lifted away on a journey to the Ospedale Maggiore by a helicopter whose gentle, balletic take-off was caught by the camera in the TV chopper.

In the paddock, there was confusion and a babble of Chinese whispers. Had Professor Watkins told Ecclestone 'It's his head' or 'He's dead'? And what had Ecclestone said to Leonardo da Silva, Senna's brother? At 2.55 p.m., thirty-eight minutes after the crash, the race resumed. Berger led for a few laps to the wild cheers of Ferrari's home crowd, and then pulled off: something wrong with the left rear corner of the car, his team said. Perhaps it was indeed so.

Schumacher won, commandingly, from Larini and Hakkinen. On the podium, still not really knowing what was going on, the three of them smiled and waved and gave the crowd a champagne shower, looking very young.

When she saw the accident, Adriane's first thought was, 'Oh good, he'll be home early tonight.' Then she realized it was serious. The radio told her that he'd regained consciousness. Her friend Luiza Braga, the wife of António, rang to say that a chartered jet was waiting on the tarmac to carry her to Bologna, a three-hour flight.

She was sitting waiting for take-off when António got through from Imola to say that Ayrton was dead. His heart had still been beating under artificial stimulation when Berger visited the hospital after the race, but there was no activity in his brain and at 6.40 p.m. the doctors decided that it was over. The jet taxied back to the terminal, and the two women drove off to the Bragas' villa in Sintra, to make new plans for a flight to São Paulo.

Berger, too, went to São Paulo, and then back to Austria, to Ratzenberger's funeral. As he crossed and recrossed the Atlantic, as he stood beside the graves of two colleagues and saw the faces of their bereaved families, he thought long and hard about retirement. On Wednesday of the following week he called a press conference.

'I earned good money,' he said. 'I was driving in good teams, I was winning races, I had pole positions . . . basically, not a lot to prove. So what is the point to take still the risk? That was my question to myself last week. But the other side is, what is the rest of your life?'

Chapter Nine

The noise on the videotape is a harsh low-pitched drone; not at all the electric howl you'd expect from a racing engine at full throttle. An ominous sound, the more so when you know what's coming next.

It's 2.17 p.m. on 1 May 1994, and the seventh lap of the San Marino Grand Prix has just begun. These pictures are coming from a camera mounted on Ayrton Senna's Williams. As he crosses the start and finish line of the Autodromo Enzo e Dino Ferrari at Imola, Senna has less than thirteen seconds to live.

Nine seconds after breaking the start-line timing beam, Senna's car enters Tamburello, at just over 190 m.p.h. The car's blue and white nose follows the trace of the bend, its nearside wheel only an inch or two from the white rumblestrip. The picture, from a camera mounted on the bodywork above the driver's left shoulder, shudders in response to ripples on the track surface, transmitted and magnified through the steel rods and carbon-fibre shell of the highly strung chassis.

The car is deep into this turn when the driver's yellow and green helmet appears at the right-hand side of the video frame. The driver is inclining his head to the left, and from the angle of the helmet he appears to be looking down. Perhaps he has seen something in his instruments. Perhaps he is peering into the rear-view mirror mounted on the left-hand side of the cockpit. The helmet jiggles.

These pictures are being beamed from the camera in Senna's car to a helicopter hovering above the circuit. Up to twenty of the twenty-six cars in the race are carrying these cameras. At any one time, four of them are sending signals to the helicopter, which relays them instantaneously down to a large grey truck parked behind the pits. In the truck, an editor chooses two or three to feed on to the event's host broadcaster, whose director will mix the pictures into coverage from his own static cameras around the circuit.

Just over eleven seconds have elapsed since the start of the lap. Now something unexpected happens, something disturbing, and suddenly the world begins to move not in seconds, as it has for the viewer at home in his armchair, but in tenths and hundredths of a second, as it does for the driver.

At 11.3 seconds there is a vibration. The car leaves the smooth curve of its trajectory. In the next tenth of a second it seems to straighten, jumping away from the line of the bend, heading across the track towards a thin strip of grass and the narrow tarmac run-off area, beyond which lies the concrete perimeter wall and a hoarding advertising Agip, the Italian national petrol company, with a single phrase, in white capital letters twenty feet high, flanked by two chequered flags: I PILOTISSIMI!

And at 11.4 seconds, with the car heading for the wall at 190 m.p.h., after four minutes and thirty-six seconds of continuous picture transmission from the camera located just behind Ayrton Senna's head, just 1.4 seconds before the fatal impact, the film ends.

The final image from Senna's car shows him heading for the wall, in line for an impact at a point just beyond the chequered flag on the Agip hoarding. He hit the wall 12.8 seconds after the start of the seventh lap, suffering a fatal head injury from a steel suspension arm which snapped when his right-hand front wheel broke off and drove its jagged end through the yellow helmet in the area of his right temple.

In the 1.4 seconds between the end of the videotape and the impact would almost certainly lie important evidence contributing towards an understanding of the cause of his death.

'The editor thought that there was no longer any interest in the picture of Senna in the lead, so he shut down the camera and switched over to the picture from Michael Schumacher's car,'

Bernie Ecclestone said many months later, giving an answer to the obvious question. 'It was a judgement call.' All the in-car cameras, and the copyright on the images they produce, are owned by the Formula One Constructors' Association, the body which Ecclestone founded and runs, and upon which, with the assistance of the lawyer Max Mosley and the entrepreneur Paddy McNally, he has built the platform for the immense prosperity of the grand prix circus. Ecclestone's understanding of the role television could play in Formula One's rise to global prominence as a major sports-entertainment package is the reason Nigel Mansell has a private jet, Ron Dennis can toss a coin over a matter of a million and a half dollars, and even design engineers earn seven-figure salaries.

But the existence of the videotape of Senna's last moments on earth took six months to come to light. FOCA's pictures from Senna's car were not being fed out live to external networks at that point during the race. Viewers around the world were watching the start of the seventh lap from the camera in Schumacher's car, a few lengths behind. If they were very alert, they saw Senna's car veer off to the right at the very instant the host broadcaster's director made the perfect natural cut to a camera positioned beyond Tamburello, looking back to see the cars leaving the curve. Mercifully for them, they did not see the moment at which the car hit the wall; the next thing they saw was the Williams ricocheting back towards the edge of the track, wheels flying into the air, the suddenly dishevelled machine coming to rest, the driver's helmet slumped motionlessly to the right.

Apart from those watching the bank of monitor screens in the big grey FOCA Communications truck which is parked close to the timing tower in the paddock at every grand prix, no one saw the pictures from Senna's car. Not until a persistent journalist, Roberto Cabrini of Brazil's TV Globo, persuaded Ecclestone to give him a copy did the outside world get a chance to see them. Until then, the pictures had been thought not to exist at all.

After Cabrini had shown the film as part of a report on the

continuing investigation into the crash, Ecclestone firmly denied ever having given the impression that there had been no pictures from Senna's car. But why had it taken so long for them to come to light? 'It didn't,' he said. 'Frank Williams had the tape two days after the crash. He phoned to ask if we had anything, and we gave it to him. If anybody else had asked, they could have had it, too.' Yet, according to Cabrini, it was only months of badgering that enabled him to break down Ecclestone's resistance.

Ecclestone – who is also vice-president of promotional affairs for the FIA, the world governing body, and therefore the man most concerned with the sport's image – tried to resolve the other mystery, the question of the missing 1.4 seconds, by explaining the FOCA editor's decision to cut away at the crucial moment in terms of the quality of the surviving tape. 'If you've seen the film,' he said, 'you'll have noticed that the picture was breaking up. It wasn't of broadcast quality.' True, as Senna comes round at the end of the sixth lap, accelerating out of the ninety-degree right-hander called Traguardo on to the straight, there is some momentary interference; but the video image has settled again before Senna approaches Tamburello. Indeed, apart from the rough growl of the engine, the final seconds have a curiously serene quality; with the empty track stretching out ahead, it is as though Senna were alone in the world.

It was easier to believe Ecclestone's contention that the editor had made a split-second decision to opt for a more obviously dramatic shot. After all, in the second he apparently chose to cut away, only Senna himself knew that something was wrong.

An early copy of the FOCA videotape went to the office of Maurizio Passarini in Bologna, a half-hour's drive from the Imola autodrome. Passarini, an investigating magistrate in his mid-thirties, was appointed in the immediate aftermath of the Imola weekend to look into both fatal accidents, Ratzenberger's as well as Senna's. His findings might lead to the absolution of all surviving parties, or to criminal charges against anyone found guilty of contributory negligence, which in effect meant either those responsible for the design and/or manufacture of the Williams car, or the managers of the Imola autodrome.

Such investigations have been held in Italy before, with inconclusive results. At Monza in 1961 Wolfgang von Trips changed direction going into the Parabolica curve without noticing the presence of Jim Clark and went flying off the road into a chain-link fence against which spectators were pressing. Fourteen of them were killed, as was von Trips. The wrecks of his Ferrari and Clark's Lotus were impounded, and the Scotsman and his team boss, Colin Chapman, left the circuit by helicopter as soon as they could. The investigation was still going on a year later, at which point Chapman, fearful of prosecution, entered his cars for the 1962 grand prix at Monza under the fictitious name of Worldwide Racing. No conclusion was ever reached. Nor was it in the case of Jochen Rindt, who died at the same track in practice for the 1970 grand prix, when it seems that a rod to the inboard front brakes of his Lotus 72 broke, just as it had in testing the previous week, in the hands of his team mate, John Miles. On both occasions the cars turned sharp left, straight off the track; in Rindt's case a fatal outcome was ensured by his preference for leaving his crotch straps undone, a comfort measure which meant that when the car hit the barrier head-on he slid forward. Rindt's car, too, was taken into custody by the authorities; it is believed to have remained in a lock-up garage at Monza for twenty years, long after the investigation had atrophied, before being quietly sold to a collector.

For all the inauspicious precedents, Maurizio Passarini was under no obligation to be anything other than completely thorough; there was no deadline for the inquiry. To assist him, he assembled a team of distinguished figures: the engineers Tommaso Carletti, a chassis specialist formerly with Minardi and Ferrari, and Mauro Forghieri, who designed Niki Lauda's championship-winning Ferraris in the mid-seventies and had recently worked on

137

the Bugatti supercar; Roberto Nosetto, a former Ferrari team manager and an official observer for the FIA; Dr Rafaele Dalmonte, a member of Italy's Olympic committee and a specialist in sports medicine; and Emmanuele Pirro, the former Benetton grand prix driver and current Italian touring car champion. The facilities of the 900-year-old University of Bologna were placed at his disposal, as were those of other research establishments, such as Pratica di Mare, the Italian military aerospace laboratory looking down from the mountain of Poggio Ballone across the Gulf of Follonica to the island of Elba.

Outsiders were kept away, including Patrick Head's team from Didcot. Head himself was allowed two ten-minute visits to the wreckage, but went away in frustration that his men, with their intimate knowledge of the car they had built and developed, could not – for perfectly sound legal reasons – be permitted to take it apart and find out what, if anything, had contributed to the tragedy. Another English racing-car designer, Adrian Reynard, had better luck. Hired by Senna's family to conduct a private investigation in parallel with the official one, he was granted half an hour with the car.

None of Senna's fellow drivers believed that he could have made a mistake: not at a corner like Tamburello, which might have been flat out but presented little challenge to the driver's skills. For a car to leave the track there, something must have gone wrong with it. From the start, there were three theories that had nothing to do with breakages or other kinds of sudden malfunction. First, Senna might have been trying so hard to stay ahead of Schumacher that, in trying to overdrive what was basically an unforgiving car, he pushed it too far; second, that his car might have picked up debris left – despite the marshals' efforts – on the start line in the wake of the Lehto/Lamy accident, upsetting its already delicate aerodynamic equilibrium; third, that his tyres had cooled down so much while running behind the safety car that even on its second lap at racing speeds the car was still running below its optimum ride-height and was bottoming on the Tamburello bumps, throwing

138

it off track. None of these possibilities seemed susceptible of absolute proof, since each depended on what might be called 'informal' data (the driver's testimony, or that of eyewitnesses) or evidence that might have been wiped away by the impact, such as debris from the earlier accident. Other theories, slower to emerge, might have a more substantial grounding.

For Passarini's analysts, the chief problem was that FW16B/2's black box, storing the data on the car's behaviour during the race, had been destroyed. The device was located on the right-hand side of the car, in between the bodywork and the carbon-fibre survival cell. Impact damage to the small battery powering the box had wiped away its memory, just as the removal of a battery from a portable car radio will erase its settings. This meant that information on the behaviour of the car's suspension, for instance, would be lost for ever.

The impounded remains of FW16B/2, its bodywork battered and ripped, lay behind the locked doors of a garage within the precincts of the autodrome. Various components were removed for inspection at Bologna University, including the steering column – which, snapped off at its root, was shown lying next to the car in photographs taken immediately after the crash. One theory, said to have its origins among the small group of people who saw the results of the first metallurgical tests, gained such wide currency that it formed the basis of a major article in the French daily sports newspaper *L'Equipe* and was broadcast around the world. This suggested that the rupture had led to the crash, rather than being among the results of it. Some said that, in the weeks leading up to the race, Senna had asked for alterations to the steering column, in order to give him more room in the cramped cockpit. It was alleged that the modifications weakened the shaft. The broken column spent many weeks at Poggio Ballone, along with certain components from the left rear suspension – which, had it failed at Tamburello, might have thrown the car into its delinquent new trajectory.

Back at Bologna, however, there was some electronic data for

139

the scientists to examine, after all. It came not from the black box, which had indeed been ruined, but from an unexpected source: the onboard memory of the engine management system, which transmitted two-second bursts of data to the Renault engineers each time the car passed the pits, the process known as downloading. In Head's words, his engineers 'piggybacked' the system, using its spare capacity to receive their own information. This data would have been downloaded at the end of the lap and then erased from the onboard memory. That indeed was what happened to the data from lap six as the car crossed the line, but the data from lap seven, all 12.8 seconds of it, was still there when the remains of FW16B/2 came to a halt. Located amidships, next to the engine whose heartbeat it was principally recording, the memory was unscathed.

Unlike the videotape, these read-outs – which came under four headings – did not end until the car hit the wall. Some of the information was unsurprising. Senna's speed was 192 m.p.h. when he entered Tamburello, and 131 m.p.h. when he hit the wall. In between, the graph suggests that his speed slowed dramatically and then accelerated again, but that is an illusion created by the fact that the speed sensors are mounted on the wheels, which locked up under heavy braking before he released them in the half-second before the impact, perhaps trying to regain control. Nor is it enlightening to know that he came right off the throttle in the space of half a second before jamming his foot back down on the accelerator pedal in the last fifth of a second; that might just have been a helpless reflex, perhaps bracing himself for the impact. The two other items, though, combined to tell a more intriguing story.

Both were related to the car's steering. The first, showing the direction and force of the steering effort, clearly demonstrated that Senna was holding the car on a steady left lock until the final instant. But the second graph, displaying the hydraulic pressure within the Williams power-steering system, is where some people came to believe the origin of the accident lay. What it shows is the pressure rising suddenly in the instant after the onset of the accident, then falling swiftly until the last half-second before impact, when it describes a crazy up-and-down pattern.

Did this indicate the sort of system failure that might have triggered the accident? Steve Nichols, an American engineer who designed the McLaren with which Senna won the 1988 world championship, was puzzled by the reading. 'If the power steering broke, you'd expect the hydraulic pressure to go straight to zero,' he said. 'It would be the same with the other reading if the accident had been started by the steering column breaking. But it's hard to tell for sure, without knowing what kind of a system they had and where the measurements were being taken within it.'

Those are the kind of details that Formula One people like to keep to themselves, or at least within the four walls of a magistrate's office. Frank Williams and Patrick Head turned all their available information over to Maurizio Passarini, and then declared themselves unavailable for further comment until the results of the inquiry were made known.

'I'm satisfied that the inquiry is being properly run,' Williams told me as the 1994 season was drawing to a close. 'He's a very serious, straightforward magistrate. I've met him and been interviewed by him, which is why I can say that he's a very honest and open individual who is insistent on finding out all the facts before he makes his decision, and he won't be rushed.'

At one point, Passarini himself hoped to announce his team's findings at the end of November, seven months after the accident. But as that time approached he issued a communiqué in which he announced a delay, pending further tests. 'The problem involves the co-ordination between experts, who are professional people with other responsibilities and obligations,' he said. 'The quality of their analysis is fundamental to the inquiry. Time is certainly marching on. There's no deadline. But we can't leave the matter for eternity.'

As Passarini's men resumed their task and argued among themselves about what their findings meant, others watched the videotape over and over again. Patrick Head said he'd seen something significant in it, but wouldn't elaborate. Steve Nichols wasn't sure. 'There are no obvious signs of panic,' he said. 'People have said that his head seemed to be bent down, that he might have been looking at something. I don't know if you can draw that conclusion. His head was bouncing up and down a lot anyway, because of the bumps.'

Might the final 1.4 seconds have told us something?

'Maybe. It's a bit like the missing eighteen minutes in the Watergate tape, isn't it?'

As the months went by, the minds of Formula One people turned away from the details of the tragedy at Imola as they became reabsorbed in their own pressing problems during a season of unparalleled turmoil and upheaval. But still the Senna accident remained a topic of conversation in and out of the paddock. Why, really, are we so concerned with the minutiae of a single accident in a sport that its practitioners necessarily accept as potentially lethal?

'Everybody wants to know what happened to the biggest figure in the sport,' Steve Nichols observed. 'But there's another thing. If there were technical reasons for the crash, the rest of us should be told. Any kind of failure – hydraulic, metallurgical, software – could tell us something. I'd just like an answer, you know?'

At the end of February, the search for the truth took a step forward when Maurizio Passarini received a 500-page report containing a technical analysis of the accidents at Imola. Its conclusions were widely leaked, and offered few surprises. Ratzenberger, the analysts wrote, appeared to have lost control as a result of damage to his front wing. As for Senna, the report concentrated on modifications to the steering of the FW16B carried out between the races at São Paulo and Imola. A fracture in one of the welds of the steering-column extension, the report suggested, was the most likely cause of the accident.

Passarini sent a copy of the findings to Didcot, from where

Patrick Head immediately issued a brisk rebuttal. 'We presented documentation within a month of the accident which pretty much showed that we couldn't have got any of the data that was recorded without the wheel being attached to the column,' he said. Head complained that his submission, and a subsequent report carefully written in layman's language, appeared to have been ignored by the investigators.

The magistrate invited the Williams team to a meeting in Bologna, but with every day that passed the prospect of a definitive verdict on the Senna accident seemed to recede.

Chapter Ten

Michael Schumacher went on to win five more races in 1994, becoming the first German driver to win the world championship, by a single point from Damon Hill. And the way he did it raised more questions about the circumstances and meaning of Ayrton Senna's death.

On that day in March when Schumacher and Verstappen were putting the finishing touches to their cars before leaving for Interlagos, Ross Brawn had leaned back in the chair of his office at the Benetton racing-car factory, a low white structure carefully blended into the gently rolling Oxfordshire countryside. He blinked behind his big round spectacles and smiled his enigmatic owlish smile as he considered his response to a question about compliance with Formula One's ban on computerized driver-aids.

Do you feel, I asked Benetton's technical director, that you're likely to stray into any of these new grey areas of illegality?

'I don't think so, no. I'm fairly confident we're kosher.'

What about the other teams?

'Well, so much depends on what results other people are getting. Ferrari, for instance. They've got a new front suspension system. Some people think it's legal, others don't. If they start to run away with the races, I'm sure the other teams would become more vociferous in their objections. But if they aren't competitive, people will tend to overlook it.'

Ten days later, nobody was thinking about Ferrari's front suspension system as Ross Brawn stood, still smiling owlishly, on the fringe of the festivities in the Benetton pit at Interlagos, waiting for Michael Schumacher to return from the podium and join the team in a glass of champagne to celebrate a conclusive victory.

Three doors up the pit lane, Ayrton Senna was contemplating what he had seen, evaluating the ease with which Schumacher had used the Benetton to blow him away. It was a thought that would preoccupy him for the last five weeks of his life. And by mid-summer, it would rival Senna's death as the defining factor of the season.

At the French Grand Prix in late June, Schumacher beat Hill off the line with a start so flawless that it hardened the suspicions lurking in many minds. This was the kind of get-away that had been seen many times in the previous two seasons, when the top teams had enjoyed the benefit of the now proscribed traction control systems and fully automatic gearboxes.

Announcing its ban on most kinds of computer-controlled devices, the FIA had been loud in its insistence that the new regulations would be regularly and strictly policed. And in July, shortly after the British Grand Prix, the FIA's technical commission produced the findings from a software analysis company, LDRA of Liverpool, which it had hired to conduct its spot checks into the computer programmes being used by three teams: Ferrari, McLaren and Benetton.

To enable these checks to be made, the teams had first to agree to surrender their source codes: the means of access to their computer programmes. Ferrari, spooked by the unpunished discovery of their use of a variation on traction control at Aida, readily complied; their cars were found to be clean. McLaren and Benetton, however, refused to produce the source codes, claiming that to do so would first compromise the commercial confidentiality and second infringe the 'intellectual copyright' of their software suppliers. When it was pointed out to them that LDRA is often enlisted by the British government to look into military software whose confidentiality is covered by the Official Secrets Act and carries weightier consequences than a silver cup, a few bottles of champagne and the further inflation of a few already oversized egos, they gave in.

Both teams were fined $100,000 for attempting to obstruct the course of justice. And, when the findings emerged, both appeared to have had something to hide. In McLaren's case it was a gearbox programme permitting automatic shifts. After much deliberating, and to the surprise of many, the FIA eventually decided that this was not illegal. But Benetton had something far more exciting up their sleeves.

When LDRA's people finally got into the B194's computer software, they discovered a hidden programme, and it was dynamite: something which allowed Schumacher to make perfect starts merely by flooring the throttle and holding it there, the computer taking over to determine the correct matching of gear-changes to engine speed, ensuring that the car reached the first corner in the least possible time, with no wheel spin or sideslip, all its energy concentrated into forward motion. Before the winter, this combination of traction control and gearbox automation would have been legal. Now, although explicitly outlawed by the regulations, it was still there. If you knew how to find it. Because it was invisible.

It took even LDRA's people a while. What you had to do was call up the software's menu of programmes, scroll down beyond the bottom line, put the cursor on an apparently blank line, press a particular key (no clues to that, either) – and, hey presto, without anything showing on the screen, the special programme was there.

They called it 'launch control', and LDRA's computer detectives also discovered the means by which the driver could activate it on his way to the starting grid. It involved a sequence of commands using the throttle and clutch pedals and the gear-shift 'paddles' under the steering wheel. Benetton couldn't deny its existence, but they did claim that it hadn't been used since it had been banned. So why was it still there, and why had its existence been so carefully disguised?

It had remained in the software, they said, because to remove it would be too difficult. The danger was that in the purging of one programme, others might become corrupted. Best to leave it be. But, so that the driver couldn't accidentally engage it and thereby unintentionally break the new rules, 'launch control' had been hidden carefully away behind a series of masking procedures.

'That's enough to make me believe they were cheating,' an experienced software programmer with another Formula One team told me. 'Look, we purged our own software of all illegal systems during the winter. I did it myself. OK, our car isn't quite as sophisticated as the Benetton. But it only took me two days. That's all. Perfectly straightforward. And the fact that they disguised it was very suspicious.'

Then he told me the most interesting thing I heard all year.

Here's what you can do, he said, if you really want to get away with something. You write an illegal programme – an offspring of traction control, say, such as a prescription for rev limits in each gear for a particular circuit – and you build into it a self-liquidating facility. This is how it works. The car leaves the pits before the race without the programme in its software. The driver stops the car on the grid, and gets out. His race engineer comes up and, as they do in the pre-race period before the grid is cleared, he plugs his little laptop computer into the car – and presses the key that downloads the illegal programme. For the next hour and a half the driver makes unrestricted use of it. Thanks to its efficiency, he wins the race. He takes his lap of honour, he drives back down the pit lane, he steers through the cheering crowds into the *parc fermé* where the scrutineers are waiting to establish the winning car's legality, and he switches off the engine. And the programme disappears, leaving not a trace of its existence.

'It's easy,' the software man said. 'In fact we use it all the time in testing, when we just want to try something out without having it hanging around to clutter up the system. And it's just about impossible to police. The FIA came round the teams early in the season, asking advice on what to do. But they're totally out of their depth here, not surprisingly. It's like crime. There's always more

148

at stake for the criminals than for the police, so the criminals are always a step ahead. It's a nightmare, really.'

The whole season was a nightmare. The deaths of Ratzenberger and Senna triggered an agony of introspection within the sport and a frenzy of comment from the world outside. What the Heysel and Hillsborough tragedies had been to soccer, Imola was to motor racing: all the hidden self-doubts, inadequacies and contradictions were brought to the surface and held up to general inspection.

At Monaco two weeks later, Karl Wendlinger lost control at high speed and crashed on the approach to the harbour-front chicane, suffering head injuries that put him into a deep coma. The drivers met to agree on a formal revival of the GPDA, the drivers' association, with Berger, Schumacher, Christian Fittipaldi and Niki Lauda as their committee. Berger remembered his own accident at Tamburello, how he asked the owners of the circuit if the concrete wall could be moved back to give more of a run-off area, and had been told, no, sorry, there's a river behind it and we can hardly move that, can we? Berger accepted their verdict. 'I was a bloody idiot,' he said five years later. Now it would be different. After Ratzenberger and Senna, all circuits would be visited by GPDA delegations in time for safety recommendations to be carried out. Suddenly the glorious history of such challenging corners as Spa's Eau Rouge and Monza's Lesmo complex was no defence in the face of the most intense wave of safety-consciousness since the mid-fifties.

At the FIA headquarters in Paris, Mosley and Ecclestone rushed to implement a series of measures designed to slow the cars down and protect the drivers from the consequences of accidents. From mid-season, there would be a mandatory use of regular pump petrol, a 50 m.p.h. limit in the pit lane and new aerodynamic restrictions; most intriguingly, all cars would have to carry a 'skidblock' bolted to their undersides – a plank made of a hard wood composite which must not be worn down beyond a certain depth. Intended to ensure that the cars maintained a certain ride height – the gap between the bottom of the car and the road surface – thereby limiting the creation of downforce, it was simultaneously acclaimed as an elegantly simple solution to a complex problem and derided as a ridiculously crude half-measure that had no place in a high-tech sport. From the start of the 1995 season the bottoms of the cars would have a 'step', making the airflow harder to manage; engine capacity would be reduced to three litres; and the bodywork would be built up around the driver's shoulders, giving protection from static and flying objects.

All this issued, essentially, from the shock waves sent out by Senna's death, as did the circus surrounding the return from America of Nigel Mansell. Disaffected with Indycar racing after his one history-making season, Mansell was readily seduced by Ecclestone into the idea of a return to Williams, taking over Senna's car. Ecclestone believed that after the retirements of Piquet, Mansell and Prost, Formula One's appeal to the mass audience could not survive the removal of Senna before the younger men – Alesi, Hakkinen, Barrichello and especially Schumacher – had been given time to establish themselves in the mind of the public. The return of the old box-office star was his solution, and won a ready response from Renault, who agreed to pay Mansell the same fee as Senna: a million dollars a race. The fact that the idea could come from Ecclestone rather than the principals of the Williams team was a powerful illustration of his influence over the sport.

At the time Ecclestone thought this up, the Williams personnel were still in their post-accident trauma. Damon Hill had told Frank Williams and Patrick Head that he wanted to take over the number one's role, and asked for their backing. They weren't so sure. Eventually David Coulthard, their regular test driver, took the seat for eight races, at a bargain fee of around £5,000 a race, with Mansell returning for the rounds at Magny-Cours, Jerez, Suzuka and Adelaide, amid a firestorm of hype that was no longer quite so urgently needed thanks to the gathering intensity of the Schumacher v Hill contest, but must nevertheless have gratified Ecclestone.

Still, if one team was at the centre of the nightmare, it was not Williams but Benetton. At Silverstone, Schumacher caused outrage when he tried to unsettle Hill, the pole man, in front of his home crowd by overtaking him twice on the parade lap, a clear act of provocation and explicitly prohibited by the rules. Coulthard, Hill's new team-mate, then stalled on the grid, leading to a repeat of the starting procedure. And on the second parade lap, Schumacher did it again. When he was shown the black flag during the race by stewards intending to subject him to a ten-second stop-and-go penalty, Schumacher ignored it for three laps – a cardinal sin which he tried to explain away by saying that he couldn't see the flag properly against the low sun. Others believed he had been encouraged to turn a blind eye by radio messages from his team, whose bosses were frantically arguing with the stewards against the penalty. At Hockenheim, the intensifying personal rivalry between Schumacher and Hill took on a darker tone when an anonymous fan telephoned the Williams driver to announce that he would be shot if he took the lead from Schumacher on the German's home track. And during that race, in a pit stop, Verstappen's Benetton was engulfed in an orange ball of flame when petrol escaped from the refuelling rig and ignited on the hot engine. The twenty-one-year-old Dutchman and his crew escaped with minor burns, a miracle to match that experienced by Berger at Imola in 1989.

But then an inspection of the rig, standard equipment supplied to FIA specifications by a French manufacturer of aircraft refuelling systems and given to the teams on the statutory basis that it be left alone, revealed that Benetton had removed a filter in order to speed up the flow of petrol. Careful calculations revealed that this might save them one second at each pit stop, an estimate that would have interested Senna, had he been alive to hear it, since that was almost exactly the margin by which Schumacher's crew had beaten his own pit workers during their two sets of refuelling stops at Interlagos in March.

And in Belgium, at the scene of his spectacular Formula One

début in 1991 and his first grand prix victory in 1992, Schumacher was disqualified from victory when the wooden plank under his car was found to have worn away by more than the permitted amount.

Whatever 'draconian' had meant to Max Mosley at the beginning of the season, the definition did not seem to apply now. Schumacher was given a two-race suspension for the black flag incident at Silverstone, while the team were fined $500,000 for their part in it, but the FIA decided that the 'best evidence' suggested that Benetton had not used the 'launch control' programme at Imola, and, to widespread astonishment, accepted as justification for the refuelling fire the team's submission that the removal of the filter had been done by a junior member acting on his own initiative, without authorization.

The bad feeling between Benetton and Williams intensified when Flavio Briatore, Benetton's managing director, persuaded Renault to break their exclusive deal with Williams and give his team the same engines in 1995, dangling before them the prospect of a link-up with Schumacher, the new superstar, in the marketing of their road cars around the world and particularly in Germany. The cold, hard decision to replace a dead superstar with a living one was made by an industrial company with an international reach, a business plan to fulfil and units of product to shift. The loss of Senna had cost Frank Williams his chief bargaining counter; now he needed Renault, on almost any terms, more than they needed him. Senna, had he lived, would never have let the French company get away with it. But then, of course, had he lived they would not have needed Michael Schumacher.

In public, too, relationships turned sour as Schumacher prepared to return from suspension for the last three races of the season. He had watched from the sidelines as Hill worked hard to close the gap by winning both the races during his absence; now he attempted to undermine the Englishman's precarious confidence by suggesting that had Senna not been killed, the Brazilian would already be world champion and would have been running rings around his team-mate, whom he described as a second-rate driver and 'a little man'. Hill spat back, giving Ecclestone the chance to pull off a cheap public-relations coup by having the pair of them mark Schumacher's comeback with a ceremonial shaking of hands in front of the pits at Jerez.

Just how cheap was revealed by Hill in his diary of the season. 'Come on, Michael,' he said as they sat on the pit-lane wall, fixing their best smiles on a couple of hundred photographers, 'let's forget all the bullshit.'

'Yes,' Schumacher replied, his smile unwavering, 'after the championship.'

They went to Adelaide for the last race of a gloomy and chaotic season with Schumacher leading Hill by one point in the contest for what would be, now and for ever, a tainted championship. Nevertheless, the showdown captured the world's imagination. Single combat. Head to head, wheel to wheel. The brash German prodigy, symbol of the economic miracle, confident of his destiny, versus the quiet Englishman, eight years older, a late developer, struggling to find his place in the scheme of things, wrestling his way out of the shadows of two world champions – his father, killed in an air crash when he was fifteen, and his late team leader.

Lap 36. Schumacher first, Hill in his wake. They approach turns three and four, a left and right. As Schumacher runs wide on the first of the two sharp bends, his right front wheel hits the wall and throws him into the middle of the track. Hill sees what has happened, and goes to pass him on the left. Schumacher, who says later that his steering was damaged, goes left, blocking Hill. His car is moving unsteadily. Hill switches, dives right, taking the inside line for turn four. Schumacher too goes for the inside, blocking Hill again. But this time the Williams is overlapping the Benetton, and the cars collide, throwing Schumacher into the air and off the track. Hill limps round to the pits, where Patrick Head sees that the left front suspension wishbone is so badly bent that it would be unsafe to continue. Replacing it would take too long.

Schumacher, parked on the grass at turn four, gets out, takes off his helmet, and is told by a marshal that Hill has retired. He is the 1994 world champion. He can't help himself. He smiles. As he walks along the edge of the track between the steel barrier and the chain-link fence, acknowledging the fans, perhaps he is already preparing the speech in which he will offer his title to the memory of Ayrton Senna.

This was 1989 and 1990 all over again. Everybody saw it, over and over again on the video replay, but although we all had an opinion no one could say what had really happened. Until we had a closer look, and slept on it, and listened to what Stewart or Lauda had to say, and looked again . . .

Schumacher's suggestion that damaged steering removed his control of the car was put in doubt by the fact that, although his car was moving erratically, it did not prevent him from effectively blocking Hill twice, first to the left and then to the right, inside a couple of seconds.

Hitting the wall certainly had some observable effect on the Benetton, which led many to question the wisdom of Hill's decision to go for the pass at the earliest opportunity. Foot off the throttle, a dab on the brake, two or three seconds to see what was going to happen next, and he would have succeeded to his father's crown.

What he did was take the racer's option. For six months he had been chasing Schumacher around the world, and the German had made few mistakes on the track. Here was one, at the season's moment of truth. It looked gift-wrapped, but all Hill's training would have told him that there are no free gifts in motor racing. He had to seize the chance. And if he had considered any other decision, he would not have been there in the first place.

Hill saw no point in making a fuss. The season had given, and it had taken away. That was something he knew about much better than Schumacher did. How could you complain about the loss of a bauble in the face of the loss of a man?

And Schumacher, too, had done what a racer would. You're in the lead. Everything is at stake. Give nothing away. Hold the line at all costs, put the car where you want to put it, let the other fellow worry about it. Some words come back: 'He left you to decide whether or not you wanted to have an accident with him.'

After all, the precedents were highly respectable. You did it, you got out, and you walked away to claim your prize. The other fellow might as well not have been there at all.

Chapter Eleven

'From the bottom of our hearts,' said Claudio Taffarel, Brazil's goalkeeper, 'we dedicate this victory to our friend Ayrton Senna. He too was heading for his fourth title.'

Brazil won the World Cup, the long awaited *tetracampeonato*, to the sound of 150 million people exploding with joy and relief. At every one of their games during USA '94, in the Rose Bowl and Stanford Stadium and the Silverdome, the yellow and green multitude carried special banners saluting the man whose fourth championship had been won in their hearts: '*Valeu campeão! Este é o seu Tetra!*'

At Estoril on the morning of the Portuguese Grand Prix, a small crowd gathered for the unveiling of a memorial erected on an infield mound, overlooking the big right-hander before the finishing straight: a white marble obelisk with a brass needle, bearing an inscription.

> *Ayrton disse um dia*
> *A morte*
> *'O dia que chegar . . .*
> *Chegou.*
> *Pode ser hoje . . .*
> *Ou daqui a 50 anos.*
> *A única coisa certa,*
> *é que ela vai chegar . . .'*

> Ayrton once said
> concerning death
> 'The day it comes,

it comes.
It could be today . . .
or not for fifty years.
The only certainty
is that it will come.'

But with Senna, no one was expecting it; in part because people had become used to the idea that racing drivers nowadays die of old age, and also because of his own particular qualities. 'He was the one driver so perfect that nobody thought anything could happen to him,' his friend Gerhard Berger said, summing up the reaction among his colleagues.

Outside the world of motor racing, the ripple of emotion extended around the world, among all types and classes. Even people who never cared much for motor racing found themselves affected. It wasn't just that a young man pre-eminent in a glamorous world had died in a tragic accident (this wasn't a James Dean job). It was suddenly clear to many people that there were other dimensions to Ayrton Senna, that the aspirations which guided his life had a meaning in terms of something other than his chosen sport. Here was a man born to an easy, privileged existence, who had chosen to make it more difficult in order to find some sort of truth for himself, because that truth could not be attained without the experience of struggle. And if, in the process, he had become the best in the world at what he did, perhaps even the best there has ever been, that had not been enough for him. One world championship or half a dozen: they may have been the target, but they were never the point.

This was why even those of us who harboured ambivalent feelings towards him in life found ourselves shaken into a reconsideration of his meaning and value, and discovering – perhaps to our surprise – how moved we were by the removal of a figure whose actions had so often been the cause of rancorous argument.

Was this the usual process of posthumous sentimentalization

accorded to dead heroes? I don't think so. When Senna was alive, he was always on the move, always thinking, always changing the equation, always making everybody else question their own positions and readjust to his movements. Only when he died were we able to look objectively at his achievements: to balance the intention, the method and the outcome. And what the read-out said was that he wouldn't be replaced, because such complexity of character and technical skill rarely coexist within a single human being.

'There is no end to the knowledge that you can get or the understanding or the peace by going deeper and deeper,' Senna once said. 'I pray regularly, not because it is a habit but because it has innovated my life. I hardly go to church because the only time I feel really good in a church is when there's nobody there.'

Like his sexual preferences or his taste in breakfast cereal, Senna's theology was his own business. But it seemed to provide him with the right kind of support for a man in his solitary trade, where many people work with great imagination and unstinting effort to provide the individual with the opportunity to put his life (and the happiness of those close to him) at hazard. 'If you have God on your side,' he said, 'everything becomes clear. I have a blessing from Him. But, of course, I can get hurt or killed, as anyone can.'

Because he chose to speak of these things, of God and morality, it was easy to get him wrong. Even easier to take a dislike to his piousness, or poke fun at his pretensions. Sports people are supposed to go no further in philosophical terms than the practised one-liner. But the more you saw of him (and, maybe, the older and wiser he grew), the easier it became to appreciate his qualities as a man. Occasionally he had lied and cheated, which made it impossible not to have mixed feelings about him. But he knew the meaning of Browning's words: 'Ah, but a man's reach should exceed his grasp,/ Or what's a heaven for?' This was his version: 'Many times I find myself in a comfortable position, and I don't feel happy about it. It is . . . an enormous desire to go further, to travel beyond my own limits.' For him the last enemy was not death, or the opponent next to him on the grid, but himself.

'I have had all my life a very strong and good education,' he once said, 'and from that I have got clear and strong principles . . . and I use these principles to move as a man and as a professional. I don't regret anything. I believe I am doing things for the right reasons. Some understand, some don't. In the end you'll never get everybody to understand, to agree and to accept . . .'

The sound of Brazilians speaking Portuguese is as close to music as human speech gets: all those soft, frictionless *zzzhhhaow* and *onnng* noises, and the falling cadences. Even in English, Senna's voice carried a special lyricism. As he collected his thoughts, mentally translated them and launched into a lucid, fantastically detailed description of some minor technical problem during a race, sometimes it made you drift away from attention to the words, the better to enjoy the music.

His willingness to confront inquisitors and deal fully and politely with them was a source of constant surprise and pleasure. After a press conference, he would often be waylaid by reporters en route to the motorhome, and would stand for an hour or more – in the sweat of his thick driving suit, at the end of an afternoon of intense physical and mental effort – until all questions had been answered in full.

Sometimes, when he was explaining why he had just squeezed Prost into the pit wall or tried to run him off the road, he could sound like a prize hypocrite. There can be no denying that he did more than anyone to bring crude dodgem tactics to Formula One, his initiative rendered relatively risk-free by the fat rubber tyres and immensely strong survival cells of the current cars. Had Fangio and Moss and Hawthorn, in their frail, spindly, unprotected vehicles, tried such things as regularly went on between Senna and Prost and Mansell, they would have killed themselves straightaway.

So Senna was able to change the mood and style of the sport, with consequences that outlived him: as the best of his time he became, for good or ill, the example for ambitious young drivers to follow.

Nor was his defence always guaranteed to win the heart of the sceptic. Once, while arguing with somebody who had done something he didn't like, he was told that he too had been known to block an opponent or two in his time. 'But I am Senna,' he said. Which sounded preposterous, until you thought about it. He was indeed Senna, and the cultivation of humility in his working life would not have taken him to the places he found. And for all the occasionally dubious nature of his intimidatory manoeuvres, it also has to be said that on many occasions his sheer brilliance deformed the behaviour of his competitors, which could hardly have been held to his account.

A rich man in a Third World country, he gave a lot of his earnings to charity, quietly. Maybe the donations – $100 million to a children's hospital in São Paulo, $75 million to an organization devoted to the health care of Indians and rubber-plantation workers in the hinterland – were conscience money. But that must have been quite a conscience. 'It cannot go on like this,' he said of his country. 'The wealthy can no longer continue to live on an island in a sea of poverty. We are all breathing the same air. People have to have a chance, a basic chance at least. A chance of education, nutrition, medical care.' The good he did in this respect was not interred with him: the Senna Foundation, run by his sister and his former associates, became the conduit for his financial legacy, concentrating its efforts on helping children.

You could forgive him a lot. On the track, for his refusal to coast, to rest on his many laurels, to take the money and, just occasionally, run a little bit slower. He lived in the present tense, looking ahead. 'I see only the future,' he said. 'The past is just data – information to consider.' Ignore the terminology. He wasn't talking about computer telemetry, but about the real flesh-and-blood proof of talent: you win something, and then go back and win it again, and again.

At Interlagos in his last season, during a practice session, I watched him in the pits, in conversation with Damon Hill and Patrick Head. Hill, who had done most of the testing on the latest car and knew much more about Williams technology than the newcomer, was doing the talking. He was describing some aspect of the FW16's behaviour, his two hands held out in front of him, palms down, moving left and right, up and down, imitating the attitude of the two sides of the car. Head was listening, occasionally saying something. But Senna was listening at some other level. Looking hard at Hill, not talking at all. Absorbing whatever information the younger man had to impart, feeding it in, making sense of it, turning it into winning data.

He wasn't impervious to fantasy. Adriane Galisteu said he talked about wanting to finish his career at Ferrari, 'even if the car is as slow as a Beetle'. It was one of the few purely romantic notions that ever escaped the privacy of his dreams. It wouldn't have happened, I guess; the Ferrari he wanted to drive was the one built under Enzo's eye. He must have fancied dropping himself into the seat once occupied by Ascari, Fangio, Gonzalez, Collins, von Trips, Surtees, Lauda and Villeneuve, but the battle of wits with the old *Ingegnere* would have been even more fun. And in that he might just have come out ahead of Fangio, whether or not he ever made it to a fifth championship, or the sixth that would have added statistical proof to the largest of all the claims made on his behalf.

'Senna was the greatest driver ever,' observed Niki Lauda, a stranger to sentimental exaggeration. 'And when someone like that is killed, you have to ask yourself what is the point of it all.'

One day, the boy told his father as they drove home, Jim Clark will be the champion of the world. That night he lay on his bed and read the race programme over and over again. For the next few years the boy traced Clark's ascent with pride. The twenty-five grand prix wins and two world championships. The historic invasion of Indianapolis.

And then, of course, Sunday 7 April 1968, the day of Clark's death in a meaningless race in Germany. His Lotus flew off the track and into the trees, for reasons nobody could ever explain. A burst tyre, perhaps. A broken suspension arm. Steering failure. He couldn't have made a mistake.

The man stands on tiptoe to reach a brown cardboard box at the top of some bookshelves. He pulls out a small pamphlet and carries it carefully back to his desk. The cover has come away from the rusting single staple; otherwise it is intact.

He looks at the results, completed in his father's familiar sloping hand. From that grey Easter Monday in 1959, his thoughts spin forward to a drizzly April afternoon in 1993, when he stood on a muddy bank and watched the yellow helmet go by.

Epilogue

'My name is Damon Hill. I am a racing driver.' The world champion leaned back in his courtroom chair, turned towards a rookery of lawyers, and awaited the first question. Three hours later, the rest of us – in the unremarkable upstairs room at the Casa Dopolavoro Imola, a social club turned into a temporary court – were still waiting for answers that might shed light on the death, just down the road, of another world champion.

This was 2 June 1997. Three years and one month after his team mate's fatal accident, Hill had been invited back to Imola to give evidence to an inquiry which, under the Italian legal system, lay in procedural terms between an inquest and a trial. Somewhere *en route*, however, he seemed to have left part of his memory behind.

A local judge, Antonio Costanzo, had been listening since late February to evidence that would determine, or so he hoped, responsibility for what happened at the start of the seventh lap of the 1994 San Marino Grand Prix. After two years of Maurizio Passarini's inquiry, and months of rumours, an examining judge, Diego Di Marco, had looked at Passarini's 700-page report and agreed to bring a charge of *omicidio colposo* – culpable homicide, the Italian version of manslaughter – against six men: Frank Williams, the team boss; Patrick Head and Adrian Newey, designers of the FW16B; Federico Bendinelli, the managing director of the company owning the Imola autodrome; Giorgio Poggi, the circuit manager; and Roland Bruynseraede, the race director. The notion of charging four of the Williams team's pit-lane personnel (chief mechanic David Brown, gearbox technician Carl Gaden, chassis man Gary Woodward and tyre mechanic Steve Coates) had been abandoned. Although none of the accused was present to hear Hill's evidence, their lawyers certainly were.

Passarini opened the proceedings with what was intended to be a searching examination of Hill, the only other man driving a Williams-Renault FW16B and sharing its secrets with Senna that day in 1994. Passarini had long since come to the conclusion that the accident had been caused by an impact fracture in the steering column, which had at some previous stage been cut, extended and rewelded in order to give Senna more room in the cramped cockpit. But the investigating magistrate was also having to explore theories that the car had been thrown off the road at 190 m.p.h. either by a fault in its power-steering system or by the combined effect of low tyre pressures and ripples on the track surface on the inside of Tamburello. A further complication had arisen a month earlier when Passarini suddenly went public with an accusation that someone had tampered with the videotape from the camera on Senna's car.

The atmosphere in the improvised courtroom was informal, verging on chaotic. There were no more than fifty people present, divided equally into lawyers, journalists and members of the public. Alongside each black-cloaked lawyer sat a glamorous and somewhat younger female assistant, affecting an elegant lack of interest. Before the hearing could begin, Hill's lawyer and business manager, Michael Breen, successfully insisted that several television crews be removed.

Sitting in front of the 36-year-old judge, whose chair was positioned under a small crucifix and a sign reading 'La legge e uguale per tutti', Hill was asked by Passarini if there had been a problem caused by a lack of space inside the cockpit of the car. Yes, Hill said, it was very tight. Did Senna have the same problem? 'I believe so.' And had they discussed it together? 'I don't remember.'

The problem in his own car, Hill continued, was to do with the amount of space between the rim of the steering wheel and the edge of the bodywork, which restricted the movement of his hands. Was that also Senna's problem? 'I can't honestly say.'

166

Dressed in a dark suit, pale blue shirt and navy and white polka dot tie, Hill was co-operative but guarded in his responses, particularly when Passarini pressed him to say exactly when the steering column had been modified. 'I don't know exactly,' he replied. 'I think it was before we went to the first test, but I can't be sure.' Before the first race of the season, then? 'I can't remember the exact date. I seem to remember it being done before we ran the car. In other words, before it went to a racetrack.' Before the beginning of the championship, then? 'Yes.'

When had he known about the modification? 'Because I don't know when it was done, I can't tell you. I was made aware that it had been done.' Did he remember who had informed him of it? 'No.' Would he confirm, then, that in 1994 the FW16B ran with power steering? 'Yes, it did.' And had the team's cars used such a system in 1993? 'I don't remember.'

At this point a degree of astonishment was in order, since one of the characteristics of a Formula One driver is an outstanding memory, a special capacity for storing and evaluating technical information. Hill might have been fired from the Williams team during the previous season amidst considerable bitterness, but any residual acrimony would hardly have erased such significant items of data, or the precise context surrounding them.

Clearly prepared for such bland responses, Passarini attempted to expose inconsistencies by reading out extracts from a statement the driver had given him during an unwitnessed interview in Imola on 16 June 1994, six weeks after the accident. According to his lawyer, Hill had never been given a copy of the statement and was therefore hearing his own three-year-old words for the first time since he uttered them. It didn't take a Perry Mason to stand up and shout 'Objection!' to that.

The supposed inconsistencies turned out to be minor and inconclusive, but there were enough of them to suggest that time had persuaded Hill to become more economical with his knowledge of the technical background. He opened up slightly on the question of the power steering, saying that the system could be activated from the cockpit, that he had been told to switch it off after Senna's accident, and that he had been given permission to switch it on again during the restarted race.

But there were further gaps in his recollection. 'In the two previous races in 1994,' Passarini asked, 'did you race with or without the power steering?'

'I honestly don't remember.'

'And at the San Marino Grand Prix, did you have a chance to talk to Senna about the car? As far as you know, did he have any reason to complain about his car?'

'I don't remember,' Hill replied – although anyone with a reasonable knowledge of contemporary Formula One would have known that by the time the Williams team reached Imola for the third race of the 1994 season, it had been apparent for weeks that the FW16 offered its drivers a surprisingly unpleasant experience. This was the sort of problem that would have occupied every waking hour of Senna and Hill, both drivers of great technical acumen, working collaboratively within the team.

Hill did talk about visiting the Williams factory a few days after the race. 'I went to a meeting with a number of the team's engineers, to try and understand the data that we had at the time, to try and find a possible reason for the accident. I came away from that meeting with the view that, on the evidence I had seen, it was difficult to explain the cause of the accident. But I had satisfied myself that there was no evidence that I could see at the time to support the theory that the steering column had broken. And it was important for me to satisfy myself on that.'

Hill talked about examining data from the steering and suspension systems during that meeting, and looking at film from the onboard camera. When he was asked about Tamburello, he replied that it wasn't a corner that the Williams drivers took in sixth gear, that it wouldn't normally be regarded as difficult for a Formula One driver, and that he hadn't experienced oversteer there himself, but that there were certainly bumps which changed the balance of the car as it travelled through the bend. 'It wasn't what you'd call an easy flat-out curve,' he observed. 'You had to concentrate. You had to be smooth with the steering.'

Passarini then devoted more than an hour to showing the court a version of the videotape from Senna's car, although lawyers for the various defendants raised objections to the legal status of a piece of footage they had apparently not been officially told about, and the court spent many minutes listening to voices raised in histrionic argument. The magistrate managed to invite Hill to comment on what he was being shown, but the driver was reluctant to commit himself, although he thought he could see that, in the seconds before the impact, Senna had twice made small steering adjustments to correct tail-slides in the corner. This, he explained, had been caused by the phenomenon called oversteer, which in this case could have resulted from low tyre pressures created by a drop in temperature when the cars ran slowly behind the safety car for five laps after the start-line accident. Low tyre pressures, Hill said, would reduce the car's ground clearance. His own FW16 had bottomed several times during the period after the safety car had left the track, releasing the field to resume at racing speed. But he could see nothing inconsistent about the images from Senna's car, although he mentioned that the version of the footage he had seen a few days after the accident had been of a better technical quality – an interesting remark in the light of Passarini's pre-hearing complaint about someone tampering with the tape.

Other lawyers questioned him. One of them, Oreste Dominioni, representing Williams and Head, asked him if he had received any communication from Patrick Head before the restart. 'I don't remember,' Hill replied. Dominioni read him a passage from his statement to Passarini: 'Before the second start, on my radio, Mr Head assured me that after an examination performed on Senna's car there was no evidence to suggest that I would suffer the same

169

problems on my car.' Do you, Dominioni asked, confirm that statement? 'Yes,' Hill replied.

Dominioni also directed him back to the question of turning off the power steering for the restart. 'I remember asking if I could turn it back on during the race,' Hill responded, 'because the steering was very heavy without it. The engineers considered it and came back to me later on the radio and said it would be safe to turn it back on. I turned it on, but by that time I'd become used to driving without it, so I turned it back off again.'

You said, Dominioni continued, that because the steering wheel became heavy, you asked for authority to turn it on. 'My arms were tired.' Does this mean that without the power steering there is a higher load on the steering wheel? 'It was heavier than it would normally be because we had adapted the steering to be quicker, which makes it heavier, thinking that we would be using power steering.'

And when he met the Williams engineers a few days after the accident, the lawyer said, had there been any suppositions advanced as a result? 'No. The only suppositions I remember are my own. When I left the factory, no conclusion had been presented to me by any of the engineers.' No discussion about finding the cause of the accident? 'I had looked at the pictures from the camera, and to me there was another kind of explanation, so it was really just a discussion about that impression.'

'Problems with the steering column,' Dominioni said, with a careful measure of asperity, 'problems with the power steering, problems with the suspension, problems with the aerodynamics, problems due to the set-up of the car, problems due to the car bottoming on the track . . . do you remember that during the meeting all these problems were discussed?'

'Yes. They were all possibilities.'

'And what was your feeling?'

'My feeling was that the car looked to me to be oversteering. There were two distinct times that it oversteered in the corner. And he did exactly what you'd expect him to do to correct it.'

Adrian Newey's lawyer, Luigi Stortoni, asked if these movements were normal or abnormal. 'The images are difficult to interpret,' Hill said. 'You have to remember that the camera moves, too, with the movement of the car.'

Roberto Causo, the FIA's lawyer, appearing on behalf of Bruynseraede, continued on the same line. Was the oversteering normal at that part of the circuit? 'No, not normal.' So why did Senna have to make two corrections? 'My own idea is that the car oversteers when it crosses the place on the circuit where there are some bumps.'

Did Hill think that low tyre pressures could be one of the potential causes of oversteering? 'When we race the cars, the temperature and pressure of the tyres is critical to the way the car handles. It affects the handling, and it affects the ride height.' So it could be the cause? 'Certainly a possibility.'

Passarini, too, returned to the question of oversteer, pointing out that Hill had not spoken of it during their meeting in Bologna, when the driver gave him the unwitnessed statement. 'I saw these pictures a week after the accident, and that was my impression. Then I came to see you in Bologna and I hadn't changed my impression. Maybe I just never mentioned the word oversteer.'

So how had his own car been behaving? 'When the safety car left the track, what I was expecting was that the car would touch the ground. It did, a little bit, in a few places, but not severely. I was driving cautiously because I knew the tyres would be cold and the pressures low.'

Passarini seemed to have run out of questions. It was one o'clock. Hill had been giving evidence all morning, give or take a couple of brief withdrawals for consultation. The judge thanked him and told him he could go. The lawyers rose, gathered their assistants, and stepped out into the streets, ready for lunch.

Through the fog of repetitive questioning and incompetent translation, you could see the angles that Passarini and the defendants' lawyers were trying to expose. But Hill remained resolute in his refusal to give an inch on any theory other than the one that Senna had crashed because low tyre pressures had caused the car to bottom on the ripples at Tamburello, throwing it off balance and into an attitude of oversteer. The only chink of fresh light emerged in his mention that the team had taken advantage of the benefits of their power-steering system by raising the gearing of the steering to make it quicker and more instantly responsive to small movements, which also made it heavier when the system was switched off. But no one asked Hill what the driver might have experienced in the event of a sudden system failure in the middle of a high-speed curve. Nor was he questioned about his reported advice to Senna, before the race, to stay away from the inside of Tamburello. ('Damon said he'd never drive there,' a team member told me long after the accident. 'If you used that bit of the track, it would save you perhaps 20 feet. Maybe Ayrton decided that he needed it.')

Others had already given their testimony: Pierluigi Martini, Michele Alboreto, Tommaso Carletti and Mauro Forghieri, who had helped Passarini and his technical advisor, Enrico Lorenzini, the head of the faculty of engineering at Bologna University, compile the report; Charlie Whiting, the head of the scrutineers; Eddie Baker and Alan Woolard of Ecclestone's Foca television team. After Hill's day in the witness box, Frank Williams also made the journey to the Casa Dopolavoro. But, as a quasi-criminal inquiry, the story was running out of steam. Passarini stuck to his conclusion, that the Williams technicians were responsible for poor design and faulty manufacture of the steering column, and that their failure represented a breach of the duty of care assumed by any manufacturer of racing cars towards the people who drive their vehicles. In the first matter, he was unable to supply definitive proof – because there could never be any such thing. In the second, he appeared to be trespassing into an area not susceptible to regulation by a legal code.

And so on 16 December 1997, three and a half years after the accident, and ten months after the commencement of the hearings, Antonio Costanzo announced that no action would be taken against any of the defendants. He quoted Article 530 of the Italian penal code, which deals with acquittals on various grounds: lack of guilt, lack of a crime, lack of proof, or a plea of justification. Williams, Head and Newey, Costanzo's deposition said, were acquitted *per non aver commesso il fatto*, because they had not committed the deed of which they were accused; the other three – Bendinelli, Poggi and Bruynseraede – *perche il fatto non sussiste*, because in their case no deed existed.

A statement issued on behalf of Williams and Head described it as 'the only possible outcome'. Passarini, however, swiftly expressed his disappointment, reasserting his belief that Head and Newey, as the team's technical chiefs, should be called to account. 'In a few seconds,' the correspondent of the *Gazzetta dello Sport* wrote, 'the judge had destroyed all the magistrate's work, disavowing two-and-a-half years of judicial inquiry, with expert opinion throughout Italy, involving the flower of professorship at the highest academic levels.' The acquittal of all six defendants, he continued, was 'like losing 6–0 at tennis or football'. According to Italian law, the magistrate had up to fifteen months in which to register an appeal against the judge's ruling.

For Leonardo Senna, nothing had changed. 'The real culprit was the wall, which was too close to the corner and didn't offer adequate protection.' Unsurprisingly, however, the world of grand prix racing expressed relief. 'A good day for Formula One,' Eddie Jordan said. Flavio Briatore, the manager of the team whose car Senna had been trying to outrun, added: 'It seems to me to be the logical outcome of an event which has gone on too long and created so much argument. Senna died in a racing accident.' Ken Tyrrell, the doyen of the paddock, commented: 'It was impossible to believe that the most successful team in Formula One, and probably the most skilful, could have made such a huge mistake.'

Damon Hill had a further reaction: 'I always believed that Williams built a car that was safe as well as fast. If I hadn't felt that way, I wouldn't have got back into the car that afternoon.'

But the certainties of Tyrrell and Hill appeared to be undermined when, exactly six months later, Costanzo published the conclusion that lay behind his decision. The balance of probability, the judge declared in the course of his 381-page document, pointed to the accident having been caused by a fracture of the rewelded steering column. For that reason, he said, the charges against Bendinelli, Poggi and Bruynseraede had been dismissed. Similarly, Frank Williams had been involved only in the commercial management of his team, and had no responsibility for the technical. Which left Head and Newey, against whom no action would be taken.

'The details of the disputed event do not allow us to state as a fact that the death of the driver was the result of a culpable infringement of a duty to prevent such events on the part of Head and Newey. The evidence as presented is not sufficient to sustain the charge or to assign to one or other of the accused the role of manufacturer or designer of the steering column. And even if one of them had taken the decision to modify it, the general circumstances would not support the accusation, and it would be necessary to show that the decision had contravened the rules of diligence. Such a demonstration was lacking, and in conclusion neither was it proved that the accused had conceived and designed the steering column.'

It was true, the judge continued, that the modification of the steering wheel was not a routine piece of work, but this did not imply that it would have been carried out by Head and Newey themselves. 'A failure to observe proper caution would have been the decision to assign the work to an unqualified technician. But the modification was carried out by a specialist. The stress fracture is not enough to raise the question of a violation of the obligation to control the work of others.'

*

Should the inquiry and the hearing, a protracted and distressing and expensive affair, have taken place at all? Inevitably, some voices, most of them British, were raised against the Italian legal system from the start. There were those who felt that Senna's death was caused by a pure racing accident, of the sort that had been happening since motor sport began, and that if you were going to subject each incident to legal scrutiny then you might as well abolish the whole sport. Others pointed to the lack of comparable fuss about the death the previous day of the far less celebrated Roland Ratzenberger; after some consideration, Passarini had concluded that there was no guilt to be detected in the circumstances of the accident that killed the Simtek driver. It didn't even take a cynic to suggest that had Ratzenberger died not on Saturday but on Sunday, not in his crash but in Senna's, and had the Brazilian not been involved, there would have been much less in the way of legal figures giving press conferences over the subsequent years.

Many Italians saw it differently, and were keen to defend the workings of their system of judicial investigation. 'In Italy,' a friend of mine said, 'as soon as there is an accidental death, the dead person is protected by law. Italian law doesn't accept that just because someone is killed doing something he enjoys, that's the end of the matter. After all, your mother may take a plane to go on holiday. You both know that planes sometimes crash. But if it did, and your mother was killed, wouldn't you want to know if the plane had been screwed together properly?'

When Max Mosley made critical remarks about the Italian legal system, suggesting that an unfavourable outcome to the proceedings might lead Formula One to withdraw from its races on Italian soil, a particularly spirited response came from Pino Allievi, the distinguished Formula One correspondent of the *Gazzetta dello Sport*. 'The truth is that in Italy there has always been motor racing, and not a single person has been jailed as a consequence of accidents, fatal or otherwise,' he wrote. 'But this does not mean that Italian magistrates should stop investigating the causes of tragedies.

Far from it. Here in Italy every citizen has the right to protection, whether his name is Senna, Williams or Rossi. Mr Mosley would do well to stick to his own business. For the moment, Italy doesn't need "advice" which is so scandalously partisan. If the English, who have always considered us to be a banana republic, will no longer come to race at Imola or Monza, so be it. Formula One will suffer much more from that decision than our civilized society.'

For the Williams team, on the other hand, the inquiry meant four years of operating with a shadow over their lives. On a banal level, it meant dealing with regular attempts to circulate rumours. Some of them indeed were regularly recirculated, such as the one about Senna having formed a habit of driving the first lap of each race without drawing breath, in order to change the balance of oxygen in his brain – something which could, according to those who propagated the story, have affected his judgement. Other rumours continued to concern the events after his death, mostly to do with who told what to whom, as in the well-sourced story that those closest to Senna were told that he was going to be all right, even after the race had been restarted.

Frank Williams and his associates and employees dealt with that by maintaining a blanket refusal to comment on anything to do with Senna or the accident – a proscription that Patrick Head, the most fascinatingly loquacious of men, infringed only once or twice, without saying anything really new. No matter how many assurances the team might be given that no one had ever been jailed in Italy as the result of a motor-racing accident, its members could be forgiven for fearing that there was a first time for everything. Mounting a defence of Williams and Head cost the team £1.5 million in legal fees.

Meanwhile Patrick Head married Betise Assumpcão, Senna's former public relations woman. Adrian Newey left the team to join McLaren for a salary believed to be in the region of £2 million a year; after a year of enforced idleness in which he served out his Williams contract, he took Ron Dennis's cars to the world drivers' and constructors' titles in his first season. And at the end of the 1998 season, the first for ten years in which his team had not won a single grand prix, Frank Williams was knighted.

As for Ayrton Senna, his memory was honoured in various ways during the years after his death. At Interlagos in 1995, the drivers paraded round the circuit on a flatbed truck, each waving a *bandeira*, as he used to do on his victory lap. In Suzuka, his presence seemed to outweigh that of the living drivers in the minds of the young Japanese fans. At Monaco, the harbour was used for the party to celebrate the launch of a rakish new Abate speedboat, with the familiar double-S on its hull. As with the T-shirts, the commemorative replica helmets, the fountain pens, the books and videos, a proportion of the profit was dedicated to the Senna Foundation, which continued with its work on behalf of Brazil's underprivileged children.

At Imola, a fine bronze statue of Senna in pensive mode was unveiled on the inside of the track at Tamburello, opposite the place at which he crashed. The precise point of his impact continued to be marked, during the week of the San Marino Grand Prix, by bunches of flowers, handwritten dedications and Brazilian flags fluttering on the wire fence. But it had grown harder to identify the exact location since the whole of Tamburello was redrawn, removing the old flat-out left-handed curve and replacing it with a big left-right chicane surrounded by acres of run-off space, incorporating vast gravel traps. The old profile of Tamburello was completely erased.

No more could you stand in the pits during practice and listen to a lone car crossing the start-line, hearing its howl hang in the air as it headed out of sight and into the woods at full throttle, imagining the sight in front of the driver as he held the car around the curve, following the concrete wall which bounded the course of the slow leaf-green waters of the Santerno. If you hadn't been there before, you couldn't imagine how such a thing might have happened.

Acknowledgements

I have cause to be grateful for the wisdom of many authors and journalists in the field of motor sport; particular debts are owed to the late Denis Jenkinson, the late Henry N. Manney III and Nigel Roebuck. In the press rooms of the modern grands prix, it is always a pleasure to hear the latest news from such erudite and generous spirits as David Tremayne, Maurice Hamilton, Alan Henry, Derick Allsop, Oliver Holt and Tim Collings. Back at the office, conversations with my friend Stephen Wood helped clarify the arguments, as well as diverting us both from the duties of the day.

Alert readers will have noticed that this is by no means the only book on the subject of Ayrton Senna. Others include *Ayrton Senna: The Hard Edge of Genius* by Christopher Hilton (Patrick Stephens, 1990; Corgi, 1991), and the same author's posthumous *Ayrton Senna* (Patrick Stephens, 1994); *Remembering Ayrton Senna* by Alan Henry (Weidenfeld and Nicolson, 1994); *Ayrton Senna: A Personal Tribute* by the photographer Keith Sutton (Osprey, 1994); *Ayrton Senna do Brasil* by Francisco Santos (Edipromo, São Paulo, 1994); *Goodbye Champion, Farewell Friend* by Karin Sturm (MRP, 1994); *Ayrton Senna: A Tribute* by Ivan Rendall (Pavilion, 1994); *My Life With Ayrton* by Adriane Galisteu (APA, 1994); and *Ayrton Senna: Prince of Formula One* by Ken Ryan (APA, 1994).

The passage in which Senna describes his mystical experience at Monaco in 1988 comes from *Grand Prix People* by Gerald Donaldson (MRP, 1990). Steve Lacy's description of the parallel experience of the musician can be found in *Improvising: Its Nature and Practice in Music* by Derek Bailey (The British Library, 1992). Enzo Ferrari's views on Fangio are from *Le mie gioie terribili* (Licinio Capelli, Bologna, 1963) and Gino Rancati's *Ferrari, lui* (Sonzogno, Turin, 1977). Fangio's views on Ferrari are from *Ma vie à 300 à l'heure* (Plon, Paris, 1961) and *Fangio: My Racing Life* (Patrick Stephens, 1990). Phil Hill's memory of passing a team mate's accident is from *The Cruel Sport* by Robert Daley (Studio Vista, 1963).

Andrew Longmore's reconstruction of Senna's last twenty-four hours in *The Times* was informative, as were the relevant passages from Denis Jenkinson's *The Racing Driver* (Batsford, 1958) and *A Story of Formula 1* (Grenville, 1960), *The Great Racing Drivers*, edited by David Hodges (Temple Press, 1966), David Tremayne's *Racers Apart* (MRP, 1991), *Inside Formula 1*, a collection of Nigel Roebuck's columns (Patrick Stephens, 1989), Timothy Collings's *Schumacher* (Bloomsbury, 1994), and Damon Hill's *Grand Prix Year* (Macmillan, 1994). Also in *The Times*, Simon Barnes has written perceptively about Senna's character.

Newspapers and periodicals consulted include *Autosport*, *Motor Sport* and *Motoring News* (UK), *L'Equipe* (France), *La Gazzetta dello Sport*, *Auto + Sport* and *Autosprint* (Italy), and *A Gazeta Esportiva*, *O Estado de São Paulo* and *Istoé* (Brazil). Special thanks go to Pino Allievi and Giancarlo Galavotti of the *Gazzetta* and Paolo Ciccarone of *Auto + Sport*.

I am particularly indebted to Ian Jack, editor of the *Independent on Sunday*, where some of these passages took their initial form as real-time journalism; to Simon O'Hagan, my first sports editor at the paper; to Alan Rusbridger, editor of the *Guardian*, and to his sports editor, Mike Averis; and to Simon Kelner, who put me on the flight to São Paulo, where Ana Cecília Americano taught me the meaning of *saudade*.